WONDERS

OF THE WORLD

NATURAL AND MAN-MADE MAJESTIES

Thank you to my parents, who gave me a taste for travel, and particularly
my mother, who passed on too soon to read about these Wonders.
—Élisabeth Dumont-Le Cornec

Library of Congress Cataloging-in-Publication Data:
Dumont-Le Cornec, Elisabeth.
Wonders of the world : natural and man-made majesties / by Elisabeth Dumont-Le Cornec ;
illustrated by Laureen Topalian and Kristel Riethmuller.
p. cm.
ISBN-13: 978-0-8109-9417-1 (hardcover)
ISBN-10: 0-8109-9417-8 (hardcover)
1. Curiosities and wonders—Pictorial works. 2. Curiosities and wonders. 3. Historic buildings—Pictorial works. 4.
Historic sites—Pictorial works. 5. Antiquities—Pictorial works. 6. Architecture—Pictorial works. 7. Natural monu-
ments—Pictorial works. 8. Natural history—Pictorial works. 9. Landscape—Pictorial works. 10. Civilization—
Miscellanea. I. Topalian, Laureen. II. Riethmuller, Kristel. III. Title.
AG243.D86 2007
031.02—dc22
2007016198

Printed and bound in Spain
10 9 8 7 6 5 4 3 2 1

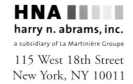

HNA
harry n. abrams, inc.
a subsidiary of La Martinière Groupe
115 West 18th Street
New York, NY 10011
www.hnabooks.com

WONDERS
OF THE WORLD

NATURAL AND MAN-MADE MAJESTIES

Élisabeth Dumont-Le Cornec

Illustrations
by Laureen Topalian
and Kristel Riethmuller

Abrams Books for Young Readers
New York

CONTENTS

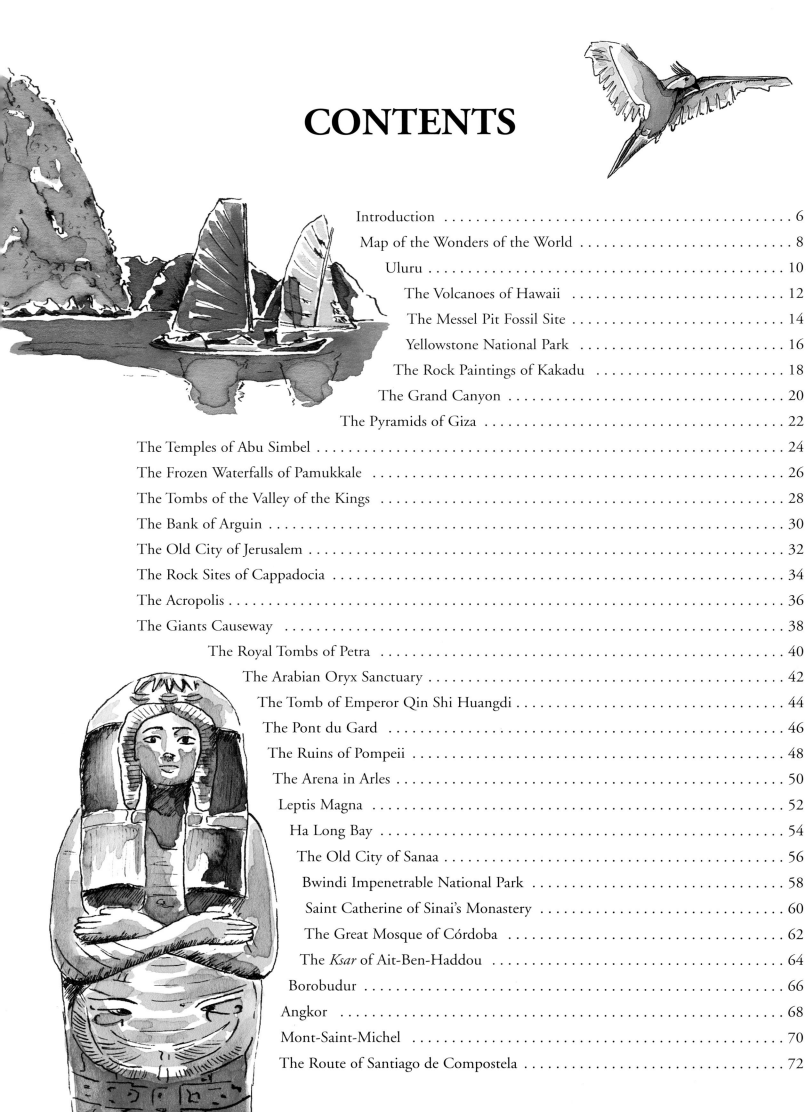

Introduction . . .

*It's hard to believe that all the wonders, all the ingenuity,
in the world is merely the result of chance and chemistry.*

René Barjavel (1911–1985)

I was seven years old when I first laid eyes on the Egyptian pyramids and the Great Sphinx, the half-human, half-lion statue standing guard at the pointed tombs of Giza. I was captivated by incredible stories of looting in the tombs, stolen mummies and pharaohs' curses, all of which sounded like the plot of a detective novel!

Imagine my amazement upon entering the tombs of the Valley of the Kings, the burial site of the pharaohs of the New Kingdom, dating from around 1500 BCE! Before my dazzled eyes rose brightly painted walls depicting the daily life of Egyptians: scenes of bird hunting, feasts of kings in their palaces, herds of cows grazing in the grass, gods with animal heads, and women in transparent tunics playing the harp. I was instantly taken by the stories of men and women going about their daily lives, the gods with their many faces, and the pharaohs captured in an unusual pose, with their shoulders facing the front and their legs and face in profile.

Given those treasures, it's no wonder that the idea of preserving endangered monuments came from Egypt. In 1956, a gigantic dam was built on the Nile River, and ancient temples started to disappear underwater. Fortunately, the decision was made to dismantle them in their entirety and rebuild them on dry land. Other countries took

notice and realized that they were responsible for their heritage and their future. Nature tells the story of the earth, and structural masterpieces tell the story of mankind. World heritage is our memory: Protecting and maintaining it helps us preserve our past and teach it to our children.

In 1972, the United Nations Educational, Scientific and Cultural Organization (UNESCO) invited countries around the world to safeguard their natural landscapes and monuments. A World Heritage List was drawn up. Today, it includes 830 sites, of which 644 are "cultural" (man-made), 162 are "natural," and 24 are both. In 2006, 182 countries signed the Convention for the Protection of World Heritage, and each year the list gets longer. During the time of antiquity, there was already a list of the Seven Wonders of the World*, monuments judged to be of exceptional interest due to the technical prowess their creators had demonstrated. Of these seven, only the Great Pyramid of Giza has stood the test of time. The rest have all disappeared.

This book is an invitation to travel the world and admire seventy-one of its present wonders. Together, they represent the vitality of our planet and the intelligence of humankind. Each one tells a different story worth preserving.

Welcome to the World of Wonders!

The world will never starve for want of wonders, but only for want of wonder.

G. K. Chesterton (1874–1936)

Map of the Wonders of the World

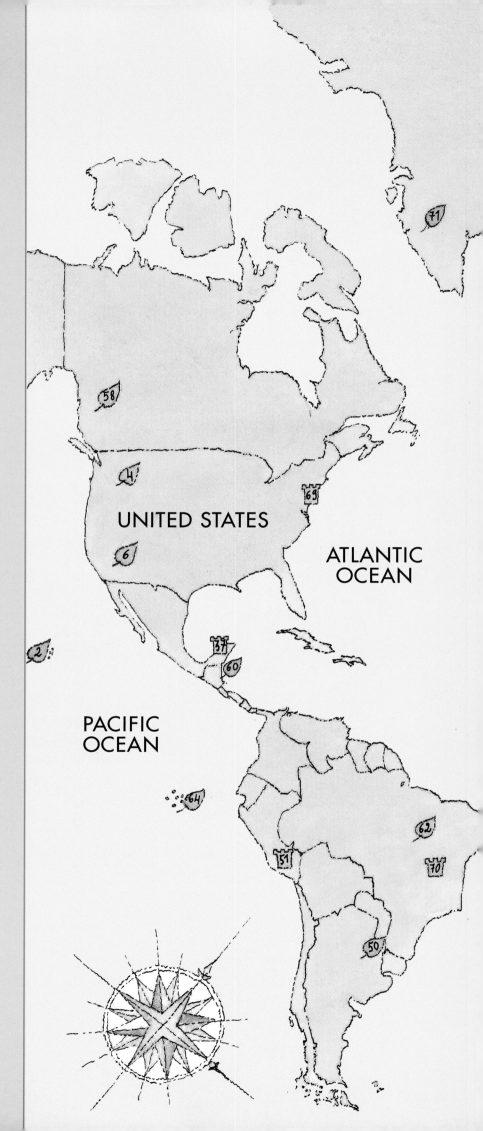

UNITED STATES

ATLANTIC OCEAN

PACIFIC OCEAN

Uluru

Since 1985, Aborigines have once again ruled over the land encompassed by the Uluru–Kata Tjuta National Park, the sacred birthplace of their Spirit Ancestors. The park is home to the largest rock on earth, which dates back 600 million years. It was named Uluru by the Aborigines.

The Aborigines are the oldest inhabitants of Australia. They believe their Spirit Ancestors created the mountains and rivers, plants and animals, and men and women, and then traveled all over Australia to build roads, create water holes, and establish laws and customs. For the Aborigines, this moment of creation is called Dreamtime.

The Snake was one of the Spirit Ancestors of Dreamtime. It crossed the barren landscape in the middle of the country where the air was so hot and the land so dry that nothing could grow or survive. The Snake decided to plant a giant seed that would grow into a giant tree in whose shadow other plants would spring up, allowing the animals to live and flourish. The Snake planted this enormous seed in the middle of the desert and then pleaded with the sky to send as much rain as it could. Sheets of rain soon fell upon the seed. But it was so big that all the rain in the world wasn't enough to germinate it. So the plains remained arid, and the sterile seed turned as hard as a rock.

For the Aborigines, the seed transformed into rock is called Uluru, and it's a sacred site, as it is where the Spirit Ancestors chose to live. Located in the Uluru–Kata Tjuta National Park, the giant red sandstone rock is the biggest monolith in the world. It measures 1,142 feet in height and 5.6 miles in circumference and takes no less than four hours to walk around. That's one enormous rock!

An Aborigine playing the didgeridoo to communicate with his ancestors

The Volcanoes of Hawaii

Hawaii's volcanoes are still active. Very active! The Kilauea volcano, depicted in the photo below, is one of the most active on the planet, having erupted no fewer than thirty-four times over the past fifty years. Its name actually means "the one that spews!" Its lava never stops flowing, constantly extending the surface of the island.

The Hawaiian Islands are a succession of active volcanoes in the Pacific Ocean. They are so frightening when they emit their red, burning lava that a multitude of Polynesian legends have attributed their origin to the gods.

In particular the legends single out the goddess of volcanoes, Pele, who constantly fought with her sister Namakaokahai, goddess of water. One day, Pele caused a volcanic eruption by hitting the ocean with her magic wand. She made a racket! Exasperated by the howls of the volcano, Namakaokahai picked a fight with her. Pele stormed off and decided to create another volcano just to annoy her more. Naturally, the quarrel between the two sisters took a turn for the worse. After many arguments, Pele hid in the crater of one of the volcanoes she had created, Kilauea, where her sister could no longer bother her.

Knowing that it was impossible to banish Pele forever, Namakaokahai proposed a peaceful solution to their conflict: Namakaokahai would allow her sister to continue living peacefully on the Big Island where she had taken refuge, but only if she agreed to repair the damage caused by the volcanoes. The deal was made, and life went back to normal . . . or almost. Nowadays, when Pele angrily taps the ground with her foot, she triggers the flow of lava!

Pele, goddess of volcanoes, created the Hawaiian Islands.

13

The Messel Pit Fossil Site

We know a lot about the prehistoric animals that lived on Earth thanks to the fossils they left in rocks. This fifty-million-year-old beetle, found in Messel, can be seen in its original colors.

The Messel Pit in Germany contains the fossils of animals and plants from tens of millions of years ago. After they died, they were covered with a type of oily shale that prevented them from decomposing. In time, they were transformed into fossils that are today encrusted in the hard surface of the rocks.

This accumulation of fossils (called a fossil site) occurred around a lake during the Eocene epoch, between fifty-seven million to thirty-six million years ago. The list of animals discovered at Messel is incredibly varied: invertebrate (mollusks and sponges), plants, and every category of vertebrate imaginable, from the oldest, fish and amphibians, to the most recent, birds and mammals. Talk about a scientific gold mine!

What's incredible is that nothing is missing from their skeletons: Even their stomachs remain intact, so we know what they ate. Some of them also have perfectly preserved fur, feathers, and skin. Certain insects have their original colored shells and certain fish their original scales. One can learn a lot from these prehistoric animals. They look quite different from the animals we know today: During the Eocene epoch, there were giant mice measuring fifteen inches in length as well as tiny horses measuring only twenty inches in length! The remains of crocodiles, snakes, and lizards were also discovered, proof that Europe once had a tropical climate. The same planet, only upside down!

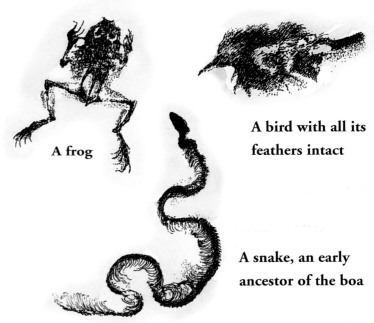

A frog

A bird with all its feathers intact

A snake, an early ancestor of the boa

Yellowstone National Park

Yellowstone is named after the yellow rock soil found in the park. A mixture of sulfur and various volcanic gases turned the rock unexpected colors.

The first fur trappers who went to Yellowstone in the early 1800s returned with so many incredible stories that everyone thought they were crazy. Some stories were told so many times, they became greatly exaggerated. Yet some were true, such as the one describing "a valley of death filled with hot springs and immense geysers" and recounting "the bison that fell into the water and was boiled like a cauldron of stew."

Yellowstone National Park contains at least three hundred geysers, jets of burning water that shoot up at intervals. The park shares its name with the Yellowstone Caldera, on which it sits, an active supervolcano that sputters warm water regularly, like a safety valve emitting steam. The park's largest geyser is called Old Faithful. It erupts every hour, reaching heights of up to 180 feet! These geysers, as well as the park's steaming pools, vertiginous waterfalls, and colored fumaroles (cracks in the rock from which volcanic gases escape), helped give Yellowstone its reputation as "the place where Hell bubbled up."

This reputation is certainly well deserved: The volcano's last eruption, which occurred more than 640,000 years ago, covered the entire north of what is now the United States with a layer of ash six and a half feet thick and provoked drastic climate change. And it may well happen again . . .

The park is teeming with wild animals, such as this bear.

The Rock Paintings of Kakadu

The rocks of Kakadu National Park in northern Australia are as old as the country's earliest inhabitants. And the paintings on the rock faces are as much as twenty thousand years old!

Did the Aborigines, the first inhabitants of Australia, invent the X-ray? You might think so after studying the painted rocks of Kakadu National Park.

Kakadu is first and foremost an incredible zoo! Fish, turtles, eels, kangaroos, emus, marine crocodiles . . . All these species were reproduced on the rock faces through a strange method that is called "X-ray art" because the drawings resemble medical X-rays. In fact, rather than a mere silhouette, each drawing features the animal's skeleton as well as its internal organs and their contents.

Next to these strange animals are drawings of spirits, or more specifically, representations of the Spirit Ancestors, who the Aborigines believe created the world. One of them, Namarrgon, the lightning man, wears stone axes on his shoulders and elbows. He is held responsible for the vicious storms that occur here during the rainy season. He creates thunder and lightning by fiercely striking his stone axes against the clouds.

Because the rock paintings cover areas so high they can't be reached from the ground, the Aborigines say that flying spirits—long, stylized figures—are their true creators. In reality, they are the handiwork of earlier Aborigines, who drew the paintings up to twenty thousand years ago!

The kangaroo, ruler of the bush, is hunted by Aborigines.

The Grand Canyon

The Grand Canyon is a gorge of spectacular proportions created by the Colorado River. It is approximately 280 miles long, between 0.5 and 18 miles wide, and, in some areas, more than a mile deep!

The Colorado River snakes its way for 280 miles between the walls of the Grand Canyon, a gigantic rocky fault whose cliffs rise more than a mile above sea level, the largest natural gorge on Earth! And it's rich with information: Its geological features and fossil record allow us to study the formation of the earth more than two billion years ago, earning it the geologists' nickname "time machine."

This site is not only interesting from a scientific perspective: It is so huge that people once thought it to be the work of the gods. When the Europeans discovered the site, they gave the cliffs divine names from every religion—from the Roman goddess Diana to the Hindu god Shiva.

The Hopi Indians, descendants of the first inhabitants of the region, have long considered the Grand Canyon a sacred place. According to their myths of the creation of the world, their ancestors formed the Grand Canyon for the sake of their people. Once they became spirits after their death, they came back to live here, which is why this site is at the heart of Hopi mythology.

Having been hunted for so long, the puma has practically disappeared from the Grand Canyon.

The Pyramids of Giza

This monumental statue, carved from limestone, is a sphinx, which has the head of a man and the body of a lion. It was built to guard the entry of the pyramid belonging to the pharaoh Cheops. According to legend, a cannon shot ripped off its nose in the ninteenth century.

Since their construction in 2,500 BCE, much has been written about the Giza pyramids of Egypt. Who erected them? Why? How? Such questions remained unanswered for years, until recently. Egyptologists now know that these pyramids were tombs commissioned by the pharaohs of the Old Kingdom.

One of the prevailing mysteries has been how the builders were able to transport so many heavy stones, often weighing as much as several tons. An incredible feat for the time! The pulley and the wheel did not exist then. Obviously, Egyptologists have been puzzled by the construction of these sacred pyramids!

Fortunately, building engineers have come to their rescue, solving the mystery. They believe that the Cheops pyramid in Giza wasn't constructed from single blocks of stone but in aggregate, meaning the limestone was reduced to powder, then mixed with water, lime (burned vegetable materials), and natron (sodium carbonate), poured into molds, and dried in the sun. Why bother cutting and transporting the stones when they could be built in one place and stacked one on top of another? And indeed, the first tests have supported this theory, proving that the Egyptians were not only great architects but also excellent chemists.

Cheops's funerary barge was buried near his pyramid.

The Temples of Abu Simbel

Was Ramses II saved from the floods? Possibly, thanks to the incredible archaeological rescue of the great temple of Abu Simbel, the sun god Ra, and the colossal statues of the pharaoh upon his throne wearing the double crown of Upper and Lower Egypt and sporting a royal beard.

In 1956, the Egyptian government decided to build a dam on the Nile River to control the rising levels of this great waterway that irrigated the country. The dam would help cultivate the surrounding arid lands for agriculture and generate electricity—a boon for the Egyptians but a loss for cultural heritage, as the construction meant that the ancient temples situated along the river would be flooded by a giant lake, 310 miles in length.

Realizing the threat, the entire world mobilized, and some fifty countries (including France, Italy, the United States, and Great Britain) allied to save these great temples.

Though many of the temples could be dismantled and transported without difficulty, the two at Abu Simbel, erected by the pharaoh Ramses II and his wife Nefertari in 1250 BCE, were partly built into the sandstone cliffs. Displacing them would be a real challenge! Yet there was no question that it had to be done: These were masterpieces of pharaoh art, particularly the larger of them—four statues, sixty-five feet high, depicted Ramses II standing guard at the entrance.

Scaffolding and cranes were used to build a mound of concrete with identical proportions to those of the sandstone containing the temples. The sculpted rock was then cut, each stone carefully numbered, and painstakingly put back together again like pieces of a puzzle. Talk about a race against the clock: It took a total of eight years of hard work to save the Abu Simbel temples from the rising waters, a goal achieved just before the opening of the dam. It was a project comparable to the great architectural feats of the pharaohs!

Reassembling the head of pharaoh Ramses II, at the entrance of his temple

The Frozen Waterfalls of Pamukkale

The frozen waterfalls of Pamukkale cover the rock with a layer of salt, glistening in the sun. The landscape is as white as a field of cotton. In Turkish, *pamukkale* actually means "cotton castle," an allusion to the castle of the region.

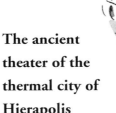

Even seen from afar, Turkey's Pamukkale dazzles its beholders with the magnificence of its white cliffs, sparkling in the sun. This curious landscape came about by way of a geological phenomenon. Pamukkale lies in the volcanic region of Anatolia, and the water that flows over the cliffs is hot, reaching temperatures of 113 degrees Fahrenheit, and rich in natural mineral salts, particularly calcium oxide. The water from the thermal springs flows down the cliffs and eventually evaporates, leaving behind mineral salt deposits.

The result? Pools and basins have formed, as well as sculptures of various shapes and sizes. The basins create a kind of frozen waterfall from which warm water also continually flows, altering the landscape. The entire mountain, as well as a large part of the valley, is covered by these solidified salts in a dazzling white.

The springs that flow here have many positive health benefits. In the second century BCE, the kings of the neighboring city Pergamum didn't miss a thing: Aware of the benefits of the warm springs, they founded Hierapolis here. This city was both a thermal bath center and a spiritual one (*hierapolis* means "holy city" in Greek). In fact, it was widely believed that the gods created this unique white landscape, a place where one could heal illnesses of the heart, arteries, skin, eyes, nerves, etc. . . .

Nowadays, Pamukkale is still known as a thermal city where visitors come to treat rheumatism and reap the benefits of the warm waters and mineral salts.

The ancient theater of the thermal city of Hierapolis

The Tombs of the Valley of the Kings

On the west bank of the Nile River, the Valley of the Kings and the Valley of the Queens served as a cemetery to pharaohs, their spouses, and the nobles of the New Kingdom (1500–1000 BCE). The walls inside the tombs are decorated with scenes of offerings and sacred texts.

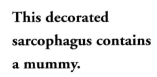
The tombs of dozens of pharaohs of ancient Egypt, as well as those of their spouses and nobles, were built into rocky cliffs to protect them from looters. Unfortunately, it didn't work. Thieves managed to steal the treasures they contained, including the mummies of the pharaohs! They stole everything, that is, except the paintings on the walls describing the lives of Egyptians and their beliefs.

When a pharaoh died, a long ritual began that involved carrying the remains by boat to the west bank of the Nile, where the sun sets, to be buried. Then came the embalming ceremony, to ensure that the body of the deceased stayed intact in the kingdom of death. The body's organs were removed and preserved in saline solution in special vases called canopic jars, which were shaped like animal heads. Next, the body was stuffed with aromatics, wrapped in tight bandages, and soaked in resin or natron (a natural sodium carbonate). The priest then performed a ritual called the Opening of the Mouth, which entailed touching the mummy's nose, eyes, ears, and mouth with an adze (a small axlike instrument) to ensure that it could breathe, see, hear, drink, and eat in the afterlife.

Finally, the mummy was placed in several stacked sarcophagi, which were painted and adorned with good-luck charms.

This decorated sarcophagus contains a mummy.

The Bank of Arguin

The Bank of Arguin is a desert of dunes on the coast of the Atlantic Ocean. The coastline is dotted with small sandy islands that serve as nesting grounds for migratory birds that stop here every year. The Imraguen tribespeople are the only remaining inhabitants.

Composed of both sand and water, Mauritania's stunning Bank of Arguin is home to a wide range of migratory birds, such as flamingos, cormorants, herons, and gulls, as well as an impressive assortment of water dwellers, such as skate, sharks, dolphins, turtles, and monk seals.

Though these sand banks may look like paradise, the climate is extremely dry: Animals merely pass through here, the area where the Sahara and the Atlantic meet, on their way to other destinations. They can't live here permanently owing to the lack of fresh water. This unique landscape comprises dunes, marshes, mangrove swamps, shallow coastal waters, and small sandy islets. Land and sea come together, with the desert encroaching more and more upon the ocean. The site is protected in order to preserve this fragile natural equilibrium.

The Imraguen, who have lived here for more than a thousand years, are the Bank of Arguin's only inhabitants. In Berber, their name means "those who fish," and indeed, fish fulfill many functions, as food, fuel, medicine, and currency.

Winter is the best season for fishing. The Imraguen spend their days casting for yellow mullets, the only fish that swim close enough to the Mauritanian shores that they can be easily caught at a short distance from the coast. As soon as an alert is sounded, the fishermen deploy their large nets in order to catch the maximum number of fish. Sometimes dolphins help to guide the fish toward the nets. Their assistance is greatly appreciated by the fishermen, especially since yellow mullets now live farther away from the shore, necessitating the use of fishing boats.

Fishing boats anchored near the Saharan coast

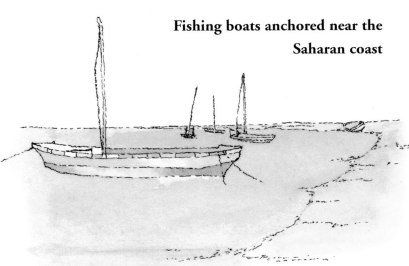

The Old City of Jerusalem

In Jerusalem, Jews, Christians, and Muslims live side by side. Obviously, Jerusalem is a holy city! Church towers, mosque domes, the Jewish temple's Wailing Wall: religious symbols here are hard to miss.

Jerusalem, in Israel, was originally a Jewish city conquered by King David, who made it the capital of the kingdom of Israel. Later, around 950 BCE, King Solomon built a temple to house the Ark of the Covenant, which contained the Ten Commandments, but the Romans destroyed it in 70 CE. Only the western part of it survived. Nowadays, Jews come to pray at the foot of the temple's remaining wall, known as the Western, or Wailing, Wall.

In the first century, Jerusalem became a holy city for Christians. It is here that Jesus of Nazareth was crucified, on Mount Calvary. According to the Gospel, Jesus, buried nearby, was resuscitated and appeared before his disciples in Jerusalem. Ever since then, the city has symbolized the death and resurrection of Christ. In 324, the Roman Empire, which occupied the city, declared Christianity the official religion. The Christians built churches on all the sites Jesus visited and made Jerusalem a sacred site of pilgrimage.

Later, Jerusalem also became a holy city for Muslims. In 638, the Arabs seized the city, and they made it the third holiest Islamic site after Mecca and Medina, where the prophet Muhammad lived. Muhammad is said to have made his departure for Paradise, as described in the Koran, at the site where the Jewish temple was built more than fifteen centuries earlier. The Dome of the Rock and the al-Aqsa Mosque were built in this same location, where Muslims now come to pray.

An Orthodox Jew praying at the foot of the Wailing Wall

The Rock Sites of Cappadocia

Cappadocia is an extraordinary site to behold! Here, in the seventh century, houses and churches were built directly into the volcanic rock, out of reach of invaders. The high-placed doors of these cavelike dwellings (right) resemble a face, with two eyes, a nose, and a mouth.

Cappadocia, in Turkey, boasts a truly unique landscape, thanks to a long geological process that began ten million years ago, when the region's volcanoes began to erupt, emitting lava, mud, ashes, and dust for several million years. Of course, there were also periods of calm, during which time the emissions settled and mixed together, creating layers three hundred to sixteen hundred feet thick! Then the climate suddenly grew cold around two million years ago, resulting in cracks in the earth's crust. Snow and rain trickled inside these cracks, creating valleys. Wind and sand slowly attacked the rocks, sculpting new cliffs, bumps, peaks, towers, points, and cones, either isolated or in groups and reaching heights of up to one hundred feet. Some of the rocks became very long and fragile.

In this bizarre landscape of colored rocks live Christian monks. In fact, monks were the first to dig into the cliffs and rocks, in order to protect their monasteries and churches from invasion. There are several hundred churches decorated with brightly colored frescoes describing the life of Jesus, the saints, and the church. In addition to these well-concealed churches, there are also the remains of underground villages where inhabitants could escape the threat of Persian or Arab invaders.

These cliffs were formed by the erosion of rocks.

The Acropolis

The Acropolis, or "high city" in Greek, is an ancient sanctuary. In its center stands Erechtheion, a temple dedicated to Athena, the patron goddess of Athens. Its entrance, the Porch of the Caryatids, is held up by columns sculpted into the figures of women with baskets on their heads.

The Acropolis of Athens, in Greece, is a flat-topped rock that rises 512 feet above sea level and measures about 900 feet long by 500 feet wide. During the time of antiquity, it was the sacred heart of the city. The impressive ruins of its temples date from the fifth century BCE and were dedicated, for the most part, to Athena, the patron goddess of the city.

According to Greek mythology, everything started with Cecrops, the first king and legendary founder of Athens, who judged a competition between Poseidon, god of the sea, and Athena, goddess of wisdom and war. It was decided that whoever gave the most useful gift to the Athenians would be declared patron of the city. The competition took place at the Acropolis. Poseidon struck the ground with his trident, and a spring of salt water sprang up. Athena, with a thrust of her lance, planted an olive tree. Cecrops preferred the olive tree because it supplied the oil used for food and illuminating the city, among other benefits. Athena therefore became patron of the city, which was named after her.

The Athenians dedicated several temples to her on the Acropolis, including the Parthenon. The Athena Polias, also called Erechtheion, is another impressive temple dedicated to her. It was built on the exact spot where the competition was supposedly held. The sacred olive tree and a well of salt water can still be seen there today. The entrance is adorned with beautiful caryatids, statues of young women dressed in long tunics that measure more than six feet in height and serve as columns for the edifice.

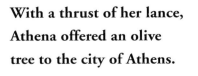

With a thrust of her lance, Athena offered an olive tree to the city of Athens.

The Giants Causeway

Spanning an area of seven square miles between the ocean and cliffs, the Giants Causeway is an array of basalt columns resulting from a sudden volcanic eruption that occurred sixty million years ago. Formed by wind and waves, these columns have unusual shapes; hence nicknames such as the Honeycomb, the Giant's Eye, and the Giant's Boot.

With its collection of some forty thousand hexagonal stones of various heights, the Giants Causeway is an arresting site. Weathered by waves and wind, it is situated along the coast of Northern Ireland.

According to legend, two rival giants lived on either side of the sea—one in Scotland, the other in Ireland. The Scottish giant cruelly taunted his Irish counterpart, insulting him and calling him a wimp. Fed up, the Irish giant challenged the Scot to a fight. But how could the Scot cross the sea? The Irish giant threw stones in the water to construct a pathway, or "causeway," between Scotland and Ireland. But when he laid eyes on his enemy, the Irish giant recoiled in fear: The Scottish giant was much bigger! He swiftly sought advice from his wife, who thought up a crazy scheme. She disguised her husband as a baby, which she presented to the Scot as her son. The Scottish giant took one look at the size of this "baby" and panicked. Terrified of the prospect of this monstrous baby's father, he ran back to Scotland, knocking down the causeway in his wake, in case the Irish giant decided to chase after him.

Geologists know that the Giants Causeway is actually the result of a volcanic eruption that occurred millions of years ago! When the lava cooled, it cracked, producing the distinctive basalt columns.

The Scottish giant called the Irish one a wimp!

The Royal Tombs of Petra

In Greek, *petra* means "rock": On this site, gigantic stone structures were carved directly into the pink sandstone cliffs. The largest of them, measuring 26 feet high, was a place of worship. It is named el-Deir, "the Monastery," because it was occupied by Christian monks.

In the fourth century BCE, Petra was the capital city of the Nabataeans, an Arabic-speaking merchant tribe. It was a major crossroads with many commercial routes passing through it, such as those of the spice, silk, ivory, and incense trades. A thriving city, Petra was encircled by mountains and situated at the end of a natural passage hollowed out by a mile-long river (now completely dried up) between rocky walls measuring up to 330 feet high.

Petra is perhaps best known for its necropolis (a gigantic cemetery) containing more than six hundred tombs carved directly into the pink sandstone walls. Most of these are royal tombs belonging to the Nabataean kings and their families, judging from their multiple stories, colonnades, and interior rooms containing the sarcophagi of the deceased. Their sculpted facades form the "wall of kings" that spans the length of the cliff.

The most famous of the tombs, the Khazneh el-Firaoun, belongs to a Nabataean king from the first century BCE. The facade, featuring columns sculpted with acanthus leaves and a statue of the Egyptian goddess Isis, mixes both Greek and Oriental decorative elements.

The Khazneh is nicknamed Treasury of the Pharaohs because legend has it that a pink sandstone urn decorating the top of the facade contained a treasure. The urn was so coveted that today it is riddled with bullet holes. But no bullet could topple it, because it was carved directly into the sandstone wall.

A caravan at rest near the Khazneh, on the spice road

The Arabian Oryx Sanctuary

Many types of rare animals live in the desert of Oman, where the Arabian oryx figures prominently. Although it was once near extinction and existed only in captivity, it now lives in the wild, alongside gazelles, Arabian wolves, and wading birds.

A herd of Arabian oryx live in the wild between the desert and the coastal hills of Oman. Today, this area is a sanctuary, a nature reserve dedicated to the protection of endangered animals such as the oryx, the largest of the Arabian antelopes. In 1972, the species had completely disappeared from the wild. Fortunately, some of them still lived in captivity. Ten years later, the animals were reintroduced into their natural habitat in Oman.

The climate here is very unique: Seasonal fogs form enough dew to support the local flora, upon which the oryx feed. Like other desert animals, oryx don't need to drink very often: The fluids contained in their food are sufficient for them to survive. Furthermore, oryx have a white coat that reflects the heat of the sun's rays, protecting them from dehydration. And the animals' black skin, underneath their white fur, creates a natural barrier to ultraviolet rays that would otherwise burn them.

But the most extraordinary feature of the oryx is its perfectly symmetrical horns. If the animal is standing in profile, it appears to have only one horn. During the time of antiquity, people believed in the existence of a single-horned animal: the unicorn. The legend of the unicorn is in fact based on the Arabian oryx, whose two horns are still impressive: Curved slightly backward, they can measure up to thirty-five inches in length and are sharp enough to be used as lethal weapons against predators.

The long-legged houbara bustard also lives in the desert.

The Tomb of Emperor Qin Shi Huangdi

These soldiers form the vanguard of an army of over seven thousand life-size terra-cotta statues buried with the Chinese Emperor Qin Shi Huangdi to keep him company in the afterlife. Dating from the third century BCE, they were discovered in Litong.

In 1974, in Litong, near the city of Xi'an in central China, archaeologists made a fascinating discovery: Life-size terra-cotta warriors! They were found in the tomb of the Chinese emperor Qin Shi Huangdi. His mausoleum, which covers an area of several acres, is filled with statues of these very lifelike soldiers wearing tunics, knee-high boots, and body armor. This army of men—on alert and ready for combat—was erected to protect its leader.

Emperor Shi Huangdi founded the Qin Dynasty and ruled China from 247 to 210 BCE. He was the first emperor of a unified China and played a major role in the history of the country. Under his reign, the country's laws, script, units of measurement, and currency were standardized, greatly simplifying the economy and the government.

Like all Chinese dignitaries of the time, Shi Huangdi designed his tomb before dying. Until the fifth century BCE, kings were buried alongside their wives, servants, and soldiers as well as their horses and dogs. They were all killed to accompany the emperor to the afterlife. Eventually, the sacrifice of humans was discontinued and was replaced by statues—first built life-size, such as the ones in Litong, and then becoming smaller and smaller, measuring a mere eight inches in the twelfth century.

Emperor Shi Huangdi got around with the help of his devoted servants.

The Pont du Gard

The Pont du Gard was part of a long aqueduct built in the first century, designed to transport water from its source to the city of Nîmes, thirty miles away. Thanks to engineering feats such as this, the Romans always had a fresh supply of water in their fountains!

For the Romans, water was an important luxury. It flowed through numerous street-corner fountains and in the homes of the wealthy. It was also vital at the thermal baths—public baths where the Romans came not only to wash but also to socialize. Water was equally important in flushing away waste and circulating through the latrines, gutters, and sewers.

In short, water brought hygiene and comfort to the lives of the Romans. The problem was that it often had to come from far away, and transporting it wasn't easy over uneven terrain. The Romans overcame this problem by building aqueducts, such as the Pont du Gard, which carried water from springs in Uzès over the Gardon River to Nîmes, thirty miles away.

The Pont du Gard is a three-level aqueduct. The third level, which is nearly 160 feet high, transported the water high above the steep Gardon riverbanks. The water flowed at a rate of forty inches per second, thanks to a perfectly precise gradient, and took less than thirty hours to make the journey from Uzès to Nîmes. That's a record for the time period! The aqueduct was built according to a very sophisticated technique and employed more than a thousand workers over a period of twenty years. It's a true Roman engineering masterpiece!

A thousand men participated in the construction of the aqueduct.

The Ruins of Pompeii

On August 24, in the year 79, the inhabitants of Pompeii were buried under layers of burning ash. Excavation of the site revealed occasional hollow spaces in the layers, left by the victims' bodies. When plaster was poured inside them, the excavators were able to re-create the forms of men, women, and children—the victims of the volcanic eruption.

The ruins at Pompeii, Italy, have given us a better understanding of Roman life in the first century, at the height of the empire. In August of the year 79, Pompeii was wiped off the map in one night, buried by the ashes and stones ejected by the eruption of the volcano Mount Vesuvius. It was as if the entire city had been suddenly petrified under the lava. Discovered by archaeologists in the eighteenth century, Pompeii is a dead but well-preserved city, with streets, houses, and magnificently decorated temples.

Everything started on August 24. The city had experienced minor ground tremors for several days prior, but people in the region had grown used to them and weren't worried. Then, on the 24th, the tremors were accompanied by a downpour of ash so fierce that some inhabitants chose to flee, jostling for space on the increasingly crowded road out of town. A threatening black cloud appeared in the sky. A Roman writer and eyewitness to the scene, Pliny the Younger, described the eruption as a towering pine tree, a vertical cloud high in the sky, emitting layer upon layer of ash. The inhabitants had no choice but to cover their eyes and noses with cloth. Those who hadn't yet escaped sought refuge in their houses to protect themselves from the pounding lapilli (small hot pumice stones). But nothing could protect them from the increasingly large stones pounding the rooftops, which eventually caved owing to the excessive weight. Huge tidal waves, provoked by the earthquakes, prevented any survivors from fleeing by sea. Soon, massive explosions of burning gas burst out of the volcano, enshrouding Pompeii, on August 25, under a twenty-foot layer of ash and killing more than two thousand people.

August 25, the year 79: The eruption of Mount Vesuvius completely destroyed the city of Pompeii.

The Arena in Arles

The arena in Arles dates back to the time of the Romans. Used to showcase games and battles between gladiators during antiquity, today the arena welcomes the biggest stars in bullfighting, which has greatly enhanced the reputation of the city.

During the time of the Gauls, Arles (Arelate) was a small, sleepy city on the Rhône delta, in the region of Camargue, where the river forks into two branches. The city's moment in the spotlight came in 49 BCE. In that year, the armies of Julius Caesar and Pompey were fighting each other for domination over the Roman world. Marseille, a city particularly coveted for its strategic position on the coast, sided with Pompey. Caesar decided to lay siege to the city and ordered Arles's shipyards to build a fleet powerful enough to defeat Pompey in the Mediterranean. Arles constructed twelve battleships in less than a month, an incredible achievement!

In 46 BCE, Caesar thanked Arles by making it an important Roman colony and a base for army veterans. Newcomers to the city constructed temples, a theater, a triumphal arch, public baths, and an arena.

Built in 80 CE, the Arles arena was inspired by the Coliseum in Rome, which had just been erected. The central stage forms a complete ellipse and is surrounded by tiers and a number of corridors for quick evacuation in case of emergency. Although not as large as the Coliseum, the arena in Arles can hold twenty-five thousand people—a sizable crowd for cheering on the gladiator battles and other spectator sports.

Bullfighters replaced gladiators in the arena.

Leptis Magna

Nowadays, Leptis Magna is a city of ruins. However, its many stone remains attest to the great civilizations that once thrived there. From the Roman era, one can see the ruins of thermal baths made of marble and decorated with statues, demonstrating the importance placed on hygiene and refinement.

Leptis Magna, a prominent city of the Roman Empire, is located on the Mediterranean coast of Libya. Septimius Severus, who became emperor in 193 CE, was born there and is credited with the transformation of the city. He built a theater, an amphitheater, a circus, a forum, thermal baths, a triumphal arch, and a basilica, lavishing the city with marble. Most important, he fixed porticoes along the sides of a popular avenue so that pedestrians could stroll along in the shade. This was quite a luxury in northern Africa, where the sun beats down mercilessly!

But the Romans were not the founders of Leptis Magna. The Phoenicians settled there first, in 1000 BCE, and made it a trading post. They were soon replaced by the Carthaginians who, in 600 BCE, transformed the city into a major port with influence throughout the Mediterranean. They shipped locally produced olive oil and other fine products to the rest of the African continent. Gold and precious stones, ivory, ostrich feathers, and even wild animals destined for Roman amphitheaters were exported from Leptis Magna.

In 146 BCE, at the end of the Punic Wars between Carthage and Rome, Leptis Magna became a Roman city, and 150 years later, it became an imperial city!

In Libya, as in Rome, one could easily spend the day lounging around the thermal baths.

Ha Long Bay

West of the Gulf of Tonkin, limestone pillars peek out of the dark water . . . Ha Long Bay is one of the most spectacular bays in the world, with hundreds of small peaks dotting the seascape. Many fishermen cast their nets from these peaks.

Vietnam's Ha Long Bay encompasses an area of 606 square miles and includes at least 1,969 islands, often nothing more than islets or rocky outcrops at close proximity to one another. Topped with vegetation, they rise between 26 and 33 feet above the water's surface. The largest of these islands, Cat Ba, measures less than 115 square miles.

According to legend, a dragon created this unusual bay. How? There are many different versions: The dragon may have descended from the mountains and started flapping its wings on the water's edge, giving rise to a new island with each motion; or, while defending the land, it may have thrown pearls into the water, which promptly turned into small islands, forming a natural barrier against invaders. It is also said that the peaks dotting the bay actually form the backbone of a dragon lying on its stomach at the bottom of the water. Scientists, however, explain the seascape as the result of constant erosion to the limestone peaks, caused by wind and water.

However it came to be, this bay is also famous for having served as a navigational reference for pirates sailing through Chinese and Vietnamese waters. A number of their boats disappeared upon approaching Ha Long Bay.

Lost junks (flat-bottomed sailing vessels) in the middle of Ha Long Bay

The Old City of Sanaa

The capital of Yemen is known throughout the world for its multistoried houses built in a similar style. Note the ocher-colored walls of rammed earth (pisé) decorated with friezes of white brick. In the distance, the minaret of a mosque towers over the houses.

Sanaa is appropriately nicknamed the "rooftop of Arabia." The city is, in fact, situated on a plateau at an altitude of 7,300 feet, making it one of the highest on the Arabian Peninsula. What's more, the tower houses lining the mountainside are six to eight stories high, making them the oldest skyscrapers in the world!

The houses were an effective way of accommodating the city's increasing population throughout the centuries. *Sanaa* actually means "fortified": The city is surrounded by walls built in the first century BCE to protect the numerous incense-carrying caravans that stopped there.

The houses stand higher than the fortified walls. But the highest points in the cityscape belong to the minarets of numerous mosques. Did you know that the oldest mosque, the Friday Mosque (corresponding to the day of rest and prayer), was built on the order of the prophet Muhammad—the founder of Islam in the seventh century—in the gardens of the Persian governor?

The building facades may all look the same, but they are actually quite different from one another, built in either brick, clay, or, more rarely, stone. The ornamentation is concentrated in the windows, which are surrounded by white gypsum, inlaid with translucent alabaster, and topped with colored windowpanes. These windowpanes, set in white, serve as decorative elements that liven up the facades. They filter in sunlight, which projects multicolored shapes on the walls and reflects in the mirrors.

The prophet Muhammad built the first mosque in Sanaa.

Bwindi Impenetrable National Park

Between the mountains and the plains, the impenetrable forest of Bwindi contains trees, plants, flowers, and animals found nowhere else on Earth. Among its diverse fauna, mountain gorillas are an endangered species and therefore extremely protected.

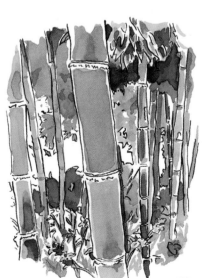

A large number of animals live in the forest of Uganda's Bwindi Impenetrable National Park: ten species of monkeys, two hundred species of butterflies, elephants, wild pigs, snakes, bats, to name just a few . . .

This African jungle, filled with hundred-year-old trees, giant bamboo, and rare flowers such as orchids, shelters some three hundred mountain gorillas—half of the world's population of this endangered species.

Mountain gorillas have thicker fur than their plains-dwelling counterparts, enabling them to live at a higher altitude and adapt to a colder climate. But they're nothing like the mean, man-eating King Kong from the movies! These primates are actually quite sociable, calm, and herbivorous. The male only beats his chest when he wants to impress his rivals and enemies. The members of this species live in a group led by a large male weighing up to 440 pounds and measuring up to 6.5 feet in height, nick-named "silverback" because its fur whitens with age.

Unfortunately, these gorillas are highly endangered. Poachers kill them for their meat, and their hands, feet, and heads are sold as good-luck charms and collector's items. Deforestation is yet another threat to their survival. It destroys their habitat and prevents them from building nests in the trees. It also forces them to live closer to humans, who transmit diseases such as measles and the flu, which can easily kill them. It's no wonder that mountain gorillas are protected and the forest is a World Heritage site!

Mountain gorillas love to eat bamboo shoots!

Saint Catherine of Sinai's Monastery

Saint Catherine of Sinai is the world's oldest Christian monastery. The saint's body is believed to have been brought here by the hands of angels. Nestled in the valley and protected by large walls, the monastery has welcomed monks since its construction in the sixth century.

Saint Catherine of Sinai's Monastery was built at an altitude of 5,150 feet, at the foot of Mount Moses (7,500 feet), in a valley between the desert and the mountains. Hidden away behind high walls, it resembles a fortress. The monastery has been in operation since it was erected by the Byzantine emperor Justinian in the sixth century. In fact, it is the oldest continuously functioning Christian monastery in the world.

The convent wasn't built here by accident. The surrounding Sinai Desert is considered holy by the three monotheistic religions: Judaism, Christianity, and Islam. According to the Bible, this is where Moses received the Ten Commandments directly from the hands of God. According to the Golden Legend, which tells the lives of saints, the monastery is also where the relics of Saint Catherine of Alexandria were brought. The pious, beautiful Alexandria native was beheaded in the fourth century for defending her Christian faith and refusing to marry a pagan emperor (who worshiped several gods). The monastery was built to house her remains.

Orthodox monks (Greek Christians) have lived here since its construction. Around twenty of them keep watch over the monastery's treasures: the church walls covered with ancient icons (images of saints), the religious wood paintings, and the library, whose collection of manuscripts is the second-most important in the Christian world, after the Vatican's. Some of the manuscripts, written entirely by hand and decorated with mosaics, date to the tenth century!

Saint Catherine was transported to Mount Sinai by the hands of angels.

The Great Mosque of Córdoba

Built by Arabs in the seventh century, the Great Mosque of Córdoba is a masterpiece of Andalusian art. In the main hall, hundreds of columns are linked together by arches made of red brick and white stone.

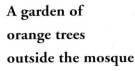

The Arabs ruled various regions of Spain between the seventh and thirteenth centuries. In 756, Prince Abd al-Rahman of the Umayyad Dynasty became the emir of Córdoba, a city in the south of the country. The city's surrounding region, Andalusia, quickly became the center of a prosperous civilization, inspired by the one the Umayyads had developed in the Orient in the previous century.

At its peak, in the tenth century, the city boasted six hundred public baths, four hundred mosques, illuminated streets, and five hundred thousand inhabitants! Though Muslims made up a majority of the population, Jews and Christians were given the right to practice their religion in exchange for a tax payment. This was very tolerant for the time!

The Great Mosque is the most symbolic of structures in Córdoba. It was built on the site of an old church previously shared by Christians and Muslims. In 785, Abd al-Rahman bought the Christian half and razed it in order to erect a mosque. After undergoing several expansions, the mosque covered an area of 3.7 acres. Held up by one thousand columns, the mosque is so huge it looks like a stone forest.

The most striking aspect of the Great Mosque is its many influences from the court of Damascus, the city where Abd al-Rahman was raised. The mosque's garden was planted with exotic flowers and trees, such as palm trees, which came from the prince's native country of Syria. The roof is also an Arab import. But the horseshoe-shaped arches and marble columns are undoubtedly Western in origin.

A garden of orange trees outside the mosque

The *Ksar* of Ait-Ben-Haddou

Established in the eleventh century, the fortified village of Ait-Ben-Haddou was named after a Berber general serving under the orders of the sultan. Though it is appreciated for its authenticity, the *ksar* is endangered due to frequent flooding . . . and film crews!

Nestled in a green oasis at the foot of the High Atlas Mountains, the *ksar* of Ait-Ben-Haddou was built directly into the red rock. A *ksar* is a fortified village made up of casbahs (fortified houses) built from adobe, a mixture of straw and earth, in the form of sun-dried bricks. The houses are several stories high and built according to the same floor plan, with a patio in the center. Families lived on the upper floors, the cattle lived on the ground floor, and the harvested crops were kept in the attic.

Founded in the eleventh century, this *ksar* was an important stopping point for caravans of merchants traveling through the Sahara Desert. However, in the past thirty years, the village has been largely deserted: Its inhabitants have moved to the other side of the *oued* (river) to live in homes with electricity and running water.

The *ksar* has slowly become a kind of ghost town, where one can go hours without seeing anyone. However, because it is so well preserved, it has served as the backdrop for many films. Crews for comedies, tragedies, and historic dramas have come to capture the stunning panorama: Alexander the Great, gladiators, Jesus, Lawrence of Arabia, Indiana Jones, and Cleopatra are among the many characters who have been filmed here, in this incredibly natural setting, between the desert and the fortified city! *Lawrence of Arabia*, directed by David Lean, was the first film shot here, in 1962. The town of Aqaba in the film is actually the *ksar* of Ait-Ben-Haddou. In 1985, a monumental red gate was built in the *ksar* to fit in with the surrounding adobe structures: It opens onto nothing, but Michael Douglas flew right through it in the film *The Jewel of the Nile*. And it's been here ever since . . .

The film *Lawrence of Arabia* was filmed in part in the *ksar*.

Borobudur

This gigantic site, built on a hill around the year 830, was discovered deep in the jungle by chance in the ninteenth century. Numerous bell-shaped pagodas (stupas) and more than eighty-two hundred feet of terraces decorate this unique pyramidal shrine . . .

In 1815, the British colonel Thomas Stamford Raffles, who governed the island of Java, discovered this shrine on a hilltop, in a magnificent landscape between rivers and volcanoes: a sanctuary, lost in the middle of the jungle, named Borobudur. Moss swallowed the stones, trees grew through entire sections of the walls, and statues toppled to the ground were covered with ash and tropical plants. The abandoned monument had practically disappeared under layers of jungle growth.

How could such a magnificent monument have been deserted? How could it have been overlooked all this time? The culprit is probably the volcano Merapi, nicknamed "mountain of fire." When it erupted in the year 919, it ejected clouds of burning ash that either killed the inhabitants or forced them to flee to surrounding areas, while covering the monument with a thick layer of volcanic ash. Until the day it was discovered . . .

The excavation of Borobudur began in the middle of the ninteenth century. The task was immense and the means complete it limited. But the shrine intrigued archaeologists because it didn't look like anything else. What purpose did it serve? They couldn't tell if it was a burial site or a temple, or whether it was Hindu or Buddhist.

After 150 years of work, the pieces of the puzzle have fallen into place. We now know that Borobudur was a shrine dating from the ninth century. The carved relief panels describe Buddhist legends and contain images showing the stages all true believers must follow to succeed in life. The monument evokes the three worlds of Buddhism: the worlds of desire, form, and formlessness. Does that mean that Borobudur served as a guide on the path toward perfection?

The shrine is adorned with statues of Buddha.

Angkor

The four giant sculpted heads above the doors of Angkor symbolize the glory of the Khmer Empire. They represent King Jayavarman VII, who decorated this capital city, which has now partially disappeared under heavy vegetation.

In 1859, the French naturalist Henri Mouhot led an exploration through regions of Siam, Laos, and Cambodia. One day, after hiking for more than three hours through dense jungle, he discovered the ruins of the imperial and religious city of Angkor: square columns carved from a single stone, rooftops in the shape of cupolas, and sculptures of the finest quality.

A popular legend tells the story of how Angkor was founded. Indra, supreme sovereign of the gods, summoned the son of the king and queen of Cambodia to heaven for a royal chore. He was to survey the celestial palaces and stables in a chariot and choose one, so that a replica could be built for his terrestrial kingdom in Cambodia. The prince modestly chose the stables. Indra sent his architect to Cambodia to build a palace in the same style as the celestial stables. The architect built the palace of Angkor Wat and painted the superb bas-reliefs adorning its walls. The prince was so pleased with the architect's handiwork that he asked him to build many others. Thus the city of Angkor was born.

Building started in the eighth century, and the city reached its peak in the twelfth century thanks to King Jayavarman VII, who defeated the Chams (an ethnic group then living in Vietnam) and established peace in Cambodia. In order to assert his sovereignty over Khmer territory, he rebuilt his capital city, making sure to incorporate his sculpted image in every new structure. What a way to make your mark as king!

The French explorer Henri Mouhot discovered Angkor in 1859.

Mont-Saint-Michel

Mont-Saint-Michel is a highly reputed pilgrimage site dedicated to the archangel Michael. It houses a Gothic abbey nicknamed the Marvel for its dazzling splendor. The mount is accessible by foot over a land bridge during low tide, which becomes submerged in water during high tide.

Why, in the eighth century, did Aubert, bishop of Avranches, build a church on an isolated rocky islet surrounded by sand at low tide and sea at high tide? Quite simply because Saint Michael himself asked him to!

Legend has it that Aubert took part in the battle between the armies of heaven and hell. The archangel Michael, who led the former, fought in a shiny suit of armor. The latter was headed by the devil in the form of a fire-spitting dragon. The battle raged for quite some time, until the archangel pierced the dragon with his spear on that isolated rocky islet between land and sea, nicknamed Mont Fall.

Following his victory, the archangel appeared to Aubert and instructed him to build a church at that sacred spot. At first, the bishop thought he was dreaming, but Saint Michael appeared to him again, this time angry. Because the bishop still hadn't obeyed his orders, during his third visit the saint burned a hole in Aubert's skull with his finger! The bishop, convinced that he wasn't dreaming, obeyed the saint and built a chapel dedicated to him in 708. Thus Mont-Saint-Michel was born, built on this site to commemorate the celestial battle and the victory of the archangel and his army of angels.

Saint Michael attacking the dragon

The Route of Santiago de Compostela

Since the Middle Ages, pilgrims have come from all over Europe to pray at the tomb of the apostle Saint James at Compostela. The pilgrimage became a sort of adventure, owing to the wolves and bandits along the route. Nowadays, the roads are more secure, but less traveled.

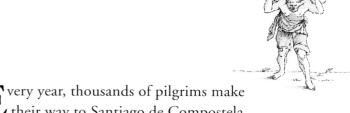

Every year, thousands of pilgrims make their way to Santiago de Compostela to pray at the shrine of Saint James; they come most often on foot, along specially marked paths. According to Christian tradition, Saint James converted Spain to Christianity in the beginning of the first century. When he returned to Jerusalem, which was then under Roman rule, he was beheaded for being Christian, a religion that was forbidden at the time. His disciples decided to carry his remains by sea to Spain to be buried. On the way there, in the middle of the sea, a knight thought long dead suddenly emerged from the water. Riding horseback, he was covered with scallop shells, earn-ing the nickname Scallop of Saint James, or in French, Coquille St. Jacques.

According to legend, when James's disciples arrived in the northwest of Spain, they were welcomed by Lupa, a pagan queen, who decided to play a trick on them. She offered them two wild bulls for their harness, which she secretly hoped would cause a disastrous accident. Imagine her surprise to see the two beasts become suddenly docile as soon as the coffin was placed on the carriage! Lupa was inspired to convert to Christianity and offered the disciples a place where the saint could be buried.

Eight hundred years later, a monk had a vision of the saint's burial place. After slashing through a pile of weeds, he discovered a marble tomb containing the preserved body of Saint James. When informed of this miracle, the ninth-century Spanish king Alfonso II declared James the patron saint of Spain and built a church to contain his relics. Since that time, the church has attracted pilgrims from all over Europe.

A Scallop of Saint James brought back from Compostela by pilgrims

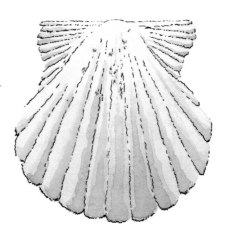

The Dazu Rock Carvings

The caves at Dazu, in China, contain thousands of statues, protected for centuries from wind and rain. That's how they maintained their bright colors, such as those seen on the Wheel of Life, which encourages man to live a virtuous life.

The Sichuan region of China is home to many caves in the mountainsides that feature elaborate rock carvings—a veritable catalog of images containing some fifty thousand statues describing the daily life of the Chinese between the ninth and thirteenth centuries! The images depict, for example, a chicken farm, a marital dispute in which a husband accuses his wife of having had too much to drink, and two cow farmers congratulating each other for having tamed a wild ox . . .

Religious scenes abound, given that a Buddhist monk built the first sculpture. Many describe the life of Buddha, the founder of Buddhism, during various moments of his life. The most famous sculpture, which has become the symbol of Dazu, is a giant reclining Buddha 102 feet long.

Another Buddhist carving, the Wheel of Life, represents the various human, animal, and divine forms of reincarnation, according to Buddhist beliefs. How a person is reincarnated depends on the merits of each person during his or her lifetime.

Elsewhere, the Eighteen Hells show what happens to those who commit sin during their lifetime. There, one finds drunken monks, men who hit their wives, and bar owners, who, once in hell, get hit repeatedly on the knees. After all, a picture is worth a thousand words!

One of the caves houses a giant reclining Buddha.

The Churches of Lalibela

In the ancient Ethiopian capital of Lalibela, a number of rock-hewn churches have attracted millions of pilgrims for the past eight hundred years. Carved from rock below ground level, the churches were designed in the shape of a cross—a completely unique design, found nowhere else in the world.

The history of the churches of Lalibela began around the year 1150, with the birth of a child in Abyssinia. Just after his birth, the baby's cradle was swarmed with a mass of bees. Since the time of the Egyptian pharaohs, the bee had been viewed as more than a mere insect—it was a symbol of royalty. As a result of this strange occurrence, the newborn's mother baptized him Lalibela, meaning "the bees proclaim their royalty." When Lalibela became an adult, he in fact took the throne. An extremely pious Christian king, he reacted to the Muslim capture of Jerusalem in 1187 by Saladin, sultan of Egypt and Syria, with anger and sadness.

As a result, Lalibela decided to build a new Jerusalem in the African desert. The town's river was named the Jordan (after the river in which Jesus was baptized), and a nearby mountain was named Mount Tabor (after the mountain upon which Jesus met his disciples and where he underwent transfiguration). Most significantly, King Lalibela built thirteen monolithic churches (from a single block of stone) into the ground. A network of tunnels was dug at the same time, linking the churches together. The structures are masterpieces of rock art. It is believed that such mastery could not have been achieved by manpower alone . . . legend has it that five hundred laborers worked on the construction of the churches by day, and an army of angels took over at night. Clearly, Lalibela is a city with divine origins!

A procession of orthodox priests

The Great Wall

Some people have claimed that the Great Wall of China can be seen from the moon. That isn't true, but the Great Wall is in fact the world's largest construction project ever completed, stretching over thirty-nine hundred miles from the border with Korea to the Gobi Desert.

The Great Wall of China, which once measured sixty-two hundred miles in length, at the end of the Han Dynasty, around the year 200, is an impressive structure to behold. At the time, it delineated a large part of the Chinese Empire's vast borders.

In the beginning, the wall was nothing more than a simple elevated causeway of dried yellow earth and gravel stretching along the northern border to protect the country from raids by barbarians. It was so effective that all subsequent Chinese sovereigns decided to extend and reinforce it. The earth walls soon became stone ramparts with watchtowers equipped to send smoke signals in times of danger.

However, no smoke signal appeared when the Mongol emperor Genghis Khan invaded China. He didn't bother trying to climb over the insurmountable obstacle in the thirteenth century, preferring instead to pay off the wall's watchtower guards. The Mongol emperor triumphantly entered the capital city of Peking without a fight.

Following his invasion, Genghis Khan took pains to maintain the integrity of this great fortification. His successors strengthened it further and soon bricks were used in its construction. The wall slowly became the impressive ramparts we admire today, with some portions of its thirty-nine hundred miles measuring twenty-six feet high and twenty feet wide. The better to keep out new invaders, as well as to publicize the immensity of the country and its power.

Despite the barrier of the Great Wall, Genghis Khan succeeded in invading China.

The Orkhon Valley

The Orkhon Valley has always attracted nomads. Nowadays, its pastures cater to herds of horses and yaks belonging to Mongolian breeders. The latter have lived here for hundreds of years in yurts—circular tents erected with wooden frameworks and lined with carpets.

The Orkhon, in Mongolia, is a river that crosses through a region of Central Asia known for its forests and steppes. It snakes through snow-capped mountains and forms waterfalls as it cascades down the mountain slopes. The Orkhon Valley is a volcanic region long inhabited by nomadic shepherds and traders, as well as hordes of conquerors.

Starting in the sixth century, a succession of nomadic tribes settled in the region, following each new invasion. Among them, Genghis Khan (1167–1227), "the supreme ruler," invaded the country in the thirteenth century and unified the various Mongol tribes under his command.

Hailed as the conqueror of Tatars and Turks, Genghis Khan is a beloved figure to Mongols, who see him as their supreme leader. He and his armies conquered China, the Turkish Empire, and parts of Russia and Bulgaria, creating an immense Mongol Empire. The city of Kharakhorum—which was chosen as the capital in 1220—became the economic and political center of the empire, a stopping place on the Silk Road and a place where ideas were exchanged and different religions were tolerated.

Few archaeological ruins remain from this famous chapter in history. The capital was entirely destroyed by successive invaders. The last of the ruins are dispersed in the Buddhist monastery of Erdene Zuu, built on the former site of Kharakhorum in 1586. Granite turtles over here, stone lions over there, parts of the palace's original walls and columns . . . only a few ruins hint at the prosperous nomadic civilization turned empire that once thrived there.

A Mongolian warrior on horseback, riding through the steppe

Chichén Itzá

Chichén Itzá, in the Yucatán Peninsula, was the religious capital of the Mayans from the ninth through the eleventh centuries. A step pyramid called el Castillo served as a place of worship of the god Quetzalcoatl, the plumed serpent. During the spring and fall equinoxes, the sun's shadow creates the illusion of Quetzalcoatl slithering up or down the stairs.

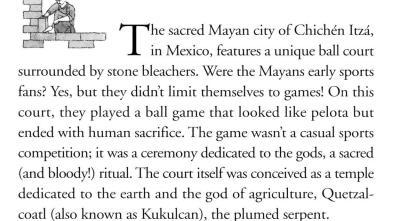

The sacred Mayan city of Chichén Itzá, in Mexico, features a unique ball court surrounded by stone bleachers. Were the Mayans early sports fans? Yes, but they didn't limit themselves to games! On this court, they played a ball game that looked like pelota but ended with human sacrifice. The game wasn't a casual sports competition; it was a ceremony dedicated to the gods, a sacred (and bloody!) ritual. The court itself was conceived as a temple dedicated to the earth and the god of agriculture, Quetzalcoatl (also known as Kukulcan), the plumed serpent.

The game involved two teams of seven players each. The idea was to hit a rubber ball (weighing as much as 6.5 pounds) to the opposing team using only one's knees, elbows, hips, or buttocks. (The players wore wooden or leather padding to protect themselves.) The object of the game was to knock the ball through a stone hoop—a difficult feat, considering the weight of the ball and the narrow size of the hoop.

The first team that managed to make a basket, despite the odds, won. But the game didn't end there. The losers were beheaded on an altar located near the ball court. This sacrifice was an offering to the gods, to win favors and ensure the changing of seasons and continued fertility of the earth. The decapitated heads were held aloft, like trophies, for all to behold.

Making a goal through the stone hoop could save lives.

The Meteora Monasteries

In the sixteenth century, twenty-four Byzantine monasteries that perched at the summit of sandstone rock pillars dominated the landscape. Renowned artists were invited to paint the frescoes describing the lives of saints and various scenes in the Bible. Nowadays, monks occupy only three of the monasteries.

A row of rocky pillars stand guard at the edge of the plain of Thessaly, in central Greece. The landscape is spectacular, particularly when one notices the eleventh- through sixteenth-century Byzantine monasteries sitting atop each rock. They are called the Meteora, which means "suspended in the air" in Greek, a reference to the monasteries' perch so high up they seem to touch the sky.

The first monks to live here chose this spot for its isolation and security. At the time, the Byzantine Empire was suffering from frequent invasions by its neighbors. The monasteries were vulnerable to looters due to the treasures they held in their attics and churches. It was an ingenious idea to build them so high up!

Though we can understand why monks sought refuge here, it is harder to understand how they got here in the first place. How did they climb the rocks, let alone transport the stones, bricks, and tiles needed to build the Byzantine churches? Some have speculated that the first hermits arrived at the summit by way of kites. In reality, the first monks made their way up the cliffs using pitons or climbing stairs built into the rock.

Once they arrived, the monks used rope ladders and hand-cranked winches to transport materials up and down the rock. From the top, a monk would lower a basket attached to a rope in which construction materials would be placed and then hoisted up to the summit. Men would arrive in the same way—by riding in a retractable basket.

Monks brought visitors up to the monasteries in baskets!

The Amiens Cathedral

The cathedral in Amiens is the largest Gothic monument in France. It is also renowned for its spectacularly sculpted facade: The statues you see gracing the center portal are the original ones built in 1236, but you must imagine them painted in bright colors, as was the custom in the Middle Ages!

Built to welcome the many pilgrims who came to pray before the head of Saint John the Baptist, the Amiens Cathedral, whose construction began in 1220, measures 475 feet long and 140 feet high. Its spire reaches an elevation of 367 feet, and its interior volume is enormous: It's two times larger than Notre-Dame Cathedral in Paris!

Starting in the twelfth century, excessively large cathedrals began to flourish across Europe. These churches are masterpieces of Gothic architecture. The pillars holding the interior aloft were connected by stone arches that intersected in the middle. This is called "rib vaulting." With this ingenious system, the vaults reached unprecedented heights and seemed to touch the sky. As the walls no longer had to hold up the ceiling, the portals were greatly expanded to let in more light in the body of the church. That explains the appearance of enormous stained-glass windows and flower-shaped rose windows.

Gothic cathedrals—with their immense size and luminosity—celebrate the greatness of God. Even their sculptures, which tell the stories of the Bible, were conceived as "books" of images to instruct the faithful, the majority of whom were illiterate at that time.

But cathedrals were expensive to build. They required significant manpower, and their construction lasted years. The cathedral in Amiens was erected thanks to donations from dyers and cloth merchants. At the time, the color Amiens blue, extracted from the leaves of woad plants grown in the region, was so popular that fabrics in this color were sold at astronomical prices as far away as Italy, bringing fortunes to their exporters!

Rib vaulting allowed cathedrals to be built to unprecedented heights.

Carcassonne

Located on a rocky hilltop, the fortified city of Carcassonne, near the border of Spain, protected the entire region from invasion. In 1408, the French king Charles VI described it as "master fortress and key sovereign of Languedoc."

Thanks to the restoration work of architect Eugène Viollet-le-Duc in the nineteenth century, Carcassonne remained a fortified city. Its outer walls are 16 to 23 feet high and more than ten feet thick. An outer rampart was added to the fortress in 1240, consisting of some thirty watchtowers with pointed rooftops. These additions made the fortress all but impregnable.

In the eighth century, Charlemagne invaded Carcassonne, when it was in the hands of Arabs from Spain. According to legend, the Arab prince Balaach was killed during the first battle. His widow, Lady Carcas, donned her deceased husband's armor and took his place at the head of the army. Many battles were fought at the foot of the fortress walls. After five years of alternating victory and defeat, Lady Carcas found herself practically alone. So she decided to make straw mannequins, which she placed at various points along the walls, to give the impression that soldiers were on guard. Charlemagne was beginning to think that this war would never end. The next day, Lady Carcas found the fattest pig she could and fed it an entire baleful of hay. She then threw the corpulent animal over the wall. Charlemagne, shocked to discover that the city had so much food remaining that it could so easily dispose of pigs, retreated. Lady Carcas blew her horn in victory. One of the warriors cried, "Carcas is sounding her horn," or in French, "Carcas sonne," and the name stuck.

According to legend, Carcassonne was named after Lady Carcas, who fiercely defended the city.

The Cliffs of Bandiagara

Composed of pisé (a mixture of earth and straw), the Dogon settlements were built on the cliffs and plateaus of Bandiagara, in Mali. Visitors must climb steep footpaths to reach them.

The Bandiagara region of Mali is famous for its breathtaking cliffs. These 125-mile-long cliffs shelter houses, granaries, shrines, and sheds that are barely distinguishable from the surrounding rock. This is the land of the Dogons. After coming here in the fourteenth century to escape the spread of Islam, the Dogon people, and their ancestral traditions, continue to thrive, in close relation with nature.

Nowadays, the Dogon people have largely abandoned their cliff dwellings in favor of homes along the plain, but their granaries have stayed put. The granaries are in fact indispensable, as the vast majority of the Dogon people grow millet, a traditional cereal crop that is a staple of their diet. Each family owns a millet granary presided over by the man of the household. The door to the granary is placed up high, out of reach of animals and thieves, and can be accessed only by way of a ladder.

The principal building of the Dogon village is the "house of words," or discussion hall, where the men meet to discuss all matters of village life. The discussion hall has a very low ceiling, making it impossible to stand without hitting one's head. This has proved useful for peacefully discussing village issues, even the most heated ones. After all, it's hard to come to blows while seated!

It's impossible to stand in the village discussion hall.

The Windmills of Kinderdijk-Elshout

The dike of Kinderdijk-Elshout features nineteen windmills made of either stone or wood. Over the centuries, they were used to pump water and drain new land for agriculture and settlement.

The windmill network of Kinderdijk-Elshout, in the Netherlands, stretches out as far as the horizon. This man-made landscape bears strong testimony to human courage and ingenuity. The windmills were used to pump water into a reservoir to drain an area of land bordering the sea. These pieces of reclaimed land are called polders. In the Netherlands, polders make up half the country's surface.

The idea of using windmills to drain water took shape after a series of devastating floods. The flood of 1421 was particularly severe: A tidal wave wiped out sixty villages, leaving few survivors. According to legend, a cat managed to keep afloat a cradle holding a baby. After the storm, the cradle washed up on a dike named Kinderdijk, which means "child's dike." This story shows to what extent the region lived in fear of flooding, since the polders consisted of land below sea level and the emergency drainage system in place at the time was utterly insufficient.

Windmills have been a feature of the landscape in the Netherlands since the Middle Ages. After the invention of electricity, however, they lost their primary function and were replaced with mechanical pumps. But the windmills in Kinderdijk-Elshout have been standing since the eighteenth century, with their sails poised to turn in the direction of the wind, just as they did in the past.

The pumps that drain polders are powered by windmills.

The Old Wharf of Bryggen

The Bryggen wharf area of Bergen dates to the Middle Ages, when it was a popular trading center. The houses here all look the same and were built following a simple floor plan: Occupants lived comfortably on the upper floors and stored their goods on the ground level.

Bryggen is one of the wharfside neighborhoods of Bergen, in Norway. The area has perfectly preserved its stretch of identical houses and churches, which appear much as they did in the fifteenth century, with their colorful wood facades. This style of architecture—typical of Nordic trading posts—also evokes the history of its traders.

In the Middle Ages, each profession had its own professional association. The association of traders in the ports of the Baltic and North seas was called the Hanse, or the Hanseatic League. It went from comprising only two cities in the thirteenth century to more than two hundred in the sixteenth century. The Hanse acquired special trading privileges for its members: protection of the traders and their goods, tax-free cargo shipping, and access to ports . . . The league also had churches built in all of its ports, whose spire, visible from afar, served as navigational markers for sailors. And the traders were given the right to recuperate their goods in the event that their ship capsized near the coast. (Before, the capsized goods automatically became the property of the monarchy.)

But sinking was extremely rare. Not only were the Hanseatic League boats the most modern of their time, but the pirates who attacked Hanse convoys were immediately sentenced to death.

Fishermen returning to the wharf of Bergen

Geirangerfjord and Nærøyfjord

The fjords have greatly inspired Nordic literature and folklore. Countless legends were born in their dark waters. Why? Because here, nature reigns supreme: Seals and porpoises swim in their depths while eagles soar high overhead.

On the western coast of Norway, in the polar regions of northern Europe, glaciers carved deep coastal valleys, which were gradually filled with water from the sea, creating the fjords. They're made up of several hundred miles of forests and cliffs, as well as vertiginous waterfalls that plunge to the waters below.

Geirangerfjord and Nærøyfjord are among the longest and deepest in the world. The sea here snakes through 125 miles of land between steep mountain slopes. Some of the snowcapped summits reach altitudes of 4,600 feet and run as deep as 1,640 feet below the water's surface. The waterfalls that flow over the cliffs have poetic names, corresponding to the country's many legends, such as the Seven Sisters, the Bridal Veil, and the Troll Wall . . .

The fjords easily trigger the imagination. They are also, according to legend, home to a veritable kingdom of trolls—devious, ugly creatures, with cucumber-shaped noses and long tails. They live in the forests and mountains and take fiendish pleasure in playing tricks on the humans they meet. What do they like best? To sow discord by tricking a man into playing a nasty practical joke on his friends. When a joke succeeds, their bursts of laughter resonate throughout the fjords.

If you want to avoid trouble, it's best to steer clear of this troll!

Ayutthaya

Based at the confluence of several rivers, within close proximity of the sea, Ayutthaya was once the capital of the Siamese Empire. It also became a holy city for Buddhism. A number of Buddha statues decorate the *prangs* (reliquary towers) and monasteries.

The ruins of the city of Ayutthaya, second capital of the empire of Siam (the former name of Thailand), attest to the past splendor of this civilization. In Sanskrit, the sacred language of India, *ayutthaya* means "undefeatable." Founded in 1350, the city was nevertheless destroyed in 1767 by the Burmese, Siam's northwest neighbors, who invaded the country.

The Uthong Dynasty established a new capital at Ayutthaya in the fourteenth century to escape an outbreak of cholera. But popular legend provides another explanation of the city's birth. One day, the king of Traitrung discovered with horror that his daughter had given birth to an illegitimate son after eating an eggplant irrigated by urine in the garden of the palace! Curses! The king summoned the princess, her baby, and the gardener, Nai Saen Pom. The god Indra, who sees all from his celestial kingdom, came to the aid of the unfortunate trio. He asked the gardener to make three wishes. Nai Saen Pom, whose name means "the man with the thousand warts," first wished for his skin growths to disappear. Then he asked to become king. And finally, he asked that his son be granted a golden cradle. As promised, Indra granted him his three wishes. The child was named Chao Uthong, "the prince of the golden cradle." Thus the Uthong Dynasty was established and a capital declared at Ayutthaya. The princes of Ayutthaya ruled the kingdom of Siam for the next four hundred years.

Floating markets on the Chao Phraya River

The Kremlin

The Kremlin, in Moscow, is a city within a city. Hidden behind imposing red walls, this citadel includes palaces, armories, and churches. The csars of Russia all made the Kremlin their home; nowadays, it is the political center of the country and the geographical heart of Moscow.

An ancient Russian legend describes the founding of Moscow and the fortress of the Kremlin. At the end of the fifteenth century, a boyar (a noble in the entourage of the Russian prince) who was out late hunting with his crew near the Moscow River decided to seek refuge in a hunting lodge for the night. When the hunting party woke up, they set off in pursuit of a wild boar, whose footprints were left in the mud. Hunting horns were sounded. Shortly thereafter, a gigantic wild boar appeared before them, ready to attack. The hunters recoiled in fear. Just as they were starting to flee, an eagle appeared from the sky and pounced on the wild animal. Curiously, the bird had two heads, and its claws looked like pitchforks. The men were more frightened of the two-headed bird than they were of the wild boar. But the eagle grasped the animal between its claws and flew to a hill at the confluence of the Moscow and Neglinnaya rivers, where it dropped the eviscerated boar. The Kremlin was built on the site of this remarkable feat.

The truth is far less romantic. Moscow was founded in 1147 by Grand Prince Yuri Dolgoruki, who built a wooden fortress on the hill, protected by forests and benefiting from the two rivers. The Russian word *kreml* actually means "fortress." Later, around the year 1490, Prince Ivan III built the brick walls surrounding the Kremlin that we see today.

The legendary two-headed eagle carrying the wild boar

101

Wooden Churches

Traditional Russian churches made of aspen wood can still be admired throughout Russia. The Church of the Transfiguration is found in Suzdal, the former capital of Russian princes.

In the year 988, Prince Vladimir I, who ruled over the first Slavic state in the east, in Kiev, converted to Christianity. In order to encourage others to follow his example, he built churches in places where idols were found—objects of adoration in ancient Slavic belief.

The northern part of Russia is covered with forests, and all the houses there are made of wood. The same goes for the churches. The carpenters of Novgorod, renowned for their talent and skills, played a major role in the construction of these churches. They acquired plenty of artistic know-how on the construction sites of this rich trading city. Some of them even participated in the construction projects of the csar, in Moscow.

These carpenters adapted the popular styles of architecture for homes and applied them to churches. The wooden houses of worship they built served as models for the stone cathedrals later built in Russia. Today, churches throughout Russia conform to the same basic style. There are tent-shaped wooden roofs and onion-domed cupolas, a standard decorative feature of the churches' exteriors. Covered with wooden shingles, these striking cupolas often entirely replace the roof and are quite stylized, appearing by the dozens around a central dome, bigger and more imposing than the rest.

An onion-shaped steeple, covered with wooden shingles

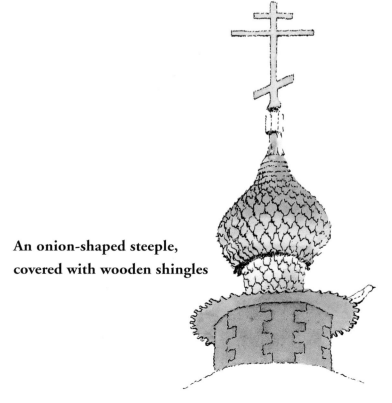

Mount Everest

Mount Everest is one of fourteen summits reaching an altitude higher than 26,246 feet in the Himalaya mountain range. Everest, at an altitude of 29,028 feet, is the highest peak. It is also the most highly esteemed among mountain climbers. The first successful climb to its summit took place on May 29, 1953.

At an elevation of 29,028 feet, Mount Everest is the highest mountain on Earth: the rooftop of the world! Beginning in the eighteenth century, many generations of mountain climbers have made attempts on the summit. More than 1,500 have made the ascent, but sadly, 150 of them never returned. Climbing Mount Everest is an adventure of extremes: glacial cold, winds whipping at 125 miles per hour, and a lack of oxygen in the thin air, which causes breathing problems. After 19,000 feet, climbers must make frequent stops to acclimate their body to the higher altitude. Obviously, making it to the summit is an exceptionally difficult task!

Access to the mount is so difficult that Everest hasn't yet divulged all its secrets. One such secret has left even scientists perplexed: that of the yeti. In Nepal, *yeti* means "magic creature," and its other name, metch-kangmi, "the filthy snowman," quickly became "the abominable snowman." However, "abominable" may have been an exaggeration, for this strange creature—half man, half ape—apparently saved a European lost in a blizzard in 1938. The yeti has remained an enigma ever since. The Tibetan government officially recognized its existence in 1961. The snowman of the Himalayas might actually be a sort of prehistoric man who has not yet evolved. It's big, with thick fur, and four toes on each foot, and it's capable of living at an altitude of 19,000 feet. Might the yeti be a cousin of modern man?

**The yeti exists!
It lives in the valleys
of the Himalayas . . .**

Saint Peter's Square in Rome

Saint Peter's Basilica is, along with the rest of Vatican City, the capital of the papacy and the Catholic Church. It is here that the martyred Saint Peter was buried in the first century. The square, demarcated by its gigantic columns, can accommodate more than fifty thousand pilgrims!

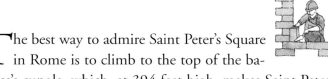

The best way to admire Saint Peter's Square in Rome is to climb to the top of the basilica's cupola, which, at 394 feet high, makes Saint Peter's the largest Catholic church in the world! Built at the spot where Saint Peter, the first pope, was martyred and buried, the basilica is a symbol of the Catholic faith.

The square surrounding the basilica is gigantic: It measures 1,115 by 787 feet. Pilgrims enter the basilica from this square. On each side of the church, numerous colonnades four columns deep form a semicircle, topped by 140 statues of saints. This long line of saints greets the faithful and guides them toward the heart of Christianity—the basilica.

In the center of the square stands an obelisk brought back from Egypt by the Romans. During antiquity, the obelisk stood in the circus of Emperor Nero, who martyred a large number of Christians. In the sixteenth century, Pope Sixtus V ordered that the obelisk be moved to its current location to memorialize these persecutions.

As soon as the first stone was lifted in this difficult and dangerous operation, the pope ordered that the crowd be silent. A bystander in the crowd noticed that the ropes were rubbing precariously against the stones and were on the verge of breaking. He yelled out that the ropes should be moistened first, so that they would slide more easily. The pope, recognizing the narrowly averted disaster, thanked the unknown person for having disobeyed his order!

One of the 140 statues of saints topping the colonnades

Iguaçu Falls

The Iguaçu Falls are a series of waterfalls averaging 230 feet in height in the middle of exceptionally beautiful nature. They were discovered by the Spanish during an expedition to the region in 1541, but the Guarani Indians had been living here for a long time prior to the discovery.

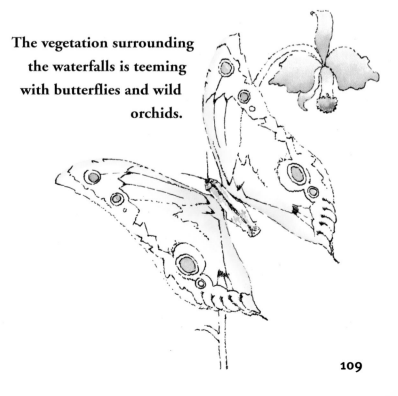

Visitors to Iguaçu are free to stroll across the many suspended footbridges located between the waterfalls and the tropical forest, where giant, multicolored butterflies, macaws, and toucans abound.

The Guarani Indians, who live in this area straddling Brazil, Argentina, and Paraguay, believe that the serpent god Mboi created the falls. Mboi was living near the Iguaçu River when he found out that his fiancée was cheating on him. Mad with rage, he whacked the ground with his tail so forcefully that it produced an enormous fissure in the Iguaçu River, giving rise to the falls. The name Iguaçu means "great waters" in the Guarani language.

The 275 successive waterfalls of Iguaçu extend over nearly 1.5 miles, at the confluence of the Iguaçu and Paraná rivers. The average height of the waterfalls is around 195 to 230 feet, but the falls at Devil's Gorge are more than 295 feet high.

Most of the falls are located in Argentina, but they can also be admired from Brazil. On the Brazilian side, the view of the falls comes with the added bonus of a rainbow in the foreground. On the Argentine side, the suspended footbridges allow visitors to see many of the waterfalls up close and to explore the diverse vegetation, such as wild orchids.

The vegetation surrounding the waterfalls is teeming with butterflies and wild orchids.

Machu Picchu

In the Incan language, *Machu Picchu* means "old peak," a name that perfectly suits the steep locale of this citadel, situated in the Andes Cordillera. What kind of city did the Incas wish to build in this isolated corner of the mountains? It remains a mystery still today . . .

Machu Picchu is in an ideal location, strategically speaking. Isolated on a rocky peak and surrounded by cliffs, it is accessible by only one road and hidden away under a dense layer of jungle, making it almost entirely invisible from the valley. Even the Spanish conquistadores who came to South America in the sixteenth century never found it, despite their numerous expeditions through the region.

It wasn't until 1911 that an American archaeologist encountered Machu Picchu, with the help of a Peruvian peasant. The discovery of this unknown Incan city caused quite a stir. Even today, Machu Picchu holds many secrets that archaeologists would like to uncover.

Built in the fifteenth century about fifty miles from the city of Cuzco, the capital of the Inca Empire, the city seems to have been abandoned rather suddenly in the mid-sixteenth century, for reasons that remain unknown. One legend attributes the desertion of Machu Picchu to the suicide of a condor. This bird, whose wingspan measures more than ten feet and which flies at an altitude of more than nineteen thousand feet, was worshiped as a god by the Incas. The Incas attached a lot of importance to signs, which they considered to be omens. But could the suicide of a condor have aroused enough fear to cause the entire population of the city to flee?

It is also unclear what purpose Machu Picchu served. Was it a religious center, a refuge for Incan aristocracy, or an astronomical observatory? The site contains a large number of temples, as well as farming terraces, public baths, residences, and an observation tower for the sun and stars.

The condor, a bird that the Incas worshiped as a god

Chaumont-sur-Loire

The fortified Chaumont castle dominates the valley of the Loire. In the sixteenth century, it served as one of the residences of the French court. The Amboise family, Catherine de Médicis, and Diane de Poitiers are just a few of its illustrious former owners.

The Chaumont castle is a medieval fortress with Renaissance airs. It belonged to the Amboise family from the twelfth through the sixteenth centuries. Like all fortified castles in the Middle Ages, it was endowed with both a massive donjon and battlements. The donjon served as a refuge in the event of attack. Each successive member of the Amboise family who made modifications to the castle kept its fortified exterior.

In 1466, a new castle replaced the old one. Though the exterior kept its fortresslike appearance, the walls overlooking the courtyard were fitted with large windows, and the chimneys and staircases inside were decorated with sculptures—additions that helped make the castle appear less austere.

Catherine de Médicis bought Chaumont for a peculiar reason in 1559, following the death of her husband, King Henry II. The French king had a mistress, Diane de Poitiers, who lived comfortably in the neighboring Chenonceau castle. When the king died, Catherine de Médicis disgraced her by forcing her to leave her beloved Chenonceau in exchange for Chaumont. Why? Perhaps to seek revenge on the woman her late husband had loved. But also because Chenonceau belonged to royalty: No king could do with it as he pleased. Therefore, Henry II should never have given it to Diane de Poitiers in the first place!

The French queen Catherine de Médicis owned the Chaumont for a period of several days!

The Jiuzhaigou Valley

The Jiuzhaigou Valley, or the "valley of nine villages" in Tibetan, is largely concealed by the forests of the Minshan mountain range encircling it. Here one finds crystal clear lakes whose colors vary depending on the underwater landscape and residues.

Once upon a time, there was a young Tibetan girl named Wonosmo on whom Heaven bestowed a golden bell filled with mystical water. Wonosmo poured the water at the foot of the Minshan Mountains, where she had planted some trees. She led a peaceful existence, living off the fruits of the trees. One day, she was attacked by a demon that stole her golden bell. After outrunning the demon, Wonosmo hid in a cave where she couldn't be found. The demon, furious at losing track of the girl, positioned itself at the entrance to the valley—a place where it was sure to run into her. In the same valley, there lived a young man who was in love with Wonosmo. Knowing where she hid, he came to her cave every day to declare his love for her. After his ten thousandth declaration of love, Wonosmo's heart stirred . . . Newly enamored, she recounted her misfortunes to him in song. The young man promised to protect her from the demon, so he attacked it. The fight lasted nine days and nine nights, but the young man didn't manage to slay the demon. Fortunately, Zaig, the spirit of the Ten Thousand Peaks, was so touched by their love that he sent all the spirits of the Jiuzhaigou to capture the demon and recover Wonosmo's bell.

The young couple, united at last, sang to their victory over the demon while ringing the bell. Suddenly, a multitude of rainbows appeared in the sky, and water spurted forth from the ground, forming 108 clear lakes. To celebrate their marriage, the spirits brought them fresh flowers, colored clouds, and rare birds and animals—all of which can still be admired today, at Jiuzhaigou Park.

The young couple ringing the golden bell

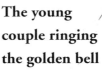

The Taj Mahal

The Taj Mahal is a mausoleum built by the Mughal emperor Shah Jahan for his wife. The mausoleum was constructed in an Indo-Muslim style by artisans from a large number of countries, including some Europeans. The emperor himself was buried in the Taj Mahal after his death in 1666.

In 1631, Mumtaz Mahal (which means "light of the palace"), wife of Mughal emperor Shah Jahan, died while giving birth to her four-teenth child. The emperor was overcome with grief at her demise, and he decided to build a mausoleum in her honor made of marble and semiprecious stones, which would take the name Taj Mahal.

Shah Jahan bought a plot of land on the edge of the Yamuna River, ordered vast quantities of marble and stone (particularly red sandstone), and recruited only the most highly qualified craftsmen for the job.

The emperor hoped that the Taj Mahal would be seen as an open door to paradise, as described in the Koran. He designed gardens with rivers flowing through them, so that his beloved wife could more easily reach immortality. The walls of the monument are engraved with Koranic verses that describe this paradise and the immortality promised to the faithful who arrive there. From the semiprecious stone flowers sculpted in the marble to the gardens, reservoirs, canals, and cypress-lined pathways that surround the mausoleum—everything was designed to evoke the image of paradise, both inside and outside the monument.

The mausoleum's many sculpted flowers were meant to evoke paradise.

Himeji-jo

Although it's a military structure, the Himeji-jo castle is far from austere. It has a highly efficient system of defense, thanks to its undulating roofs on each floor and its towers of various sizes and heights. This great feudal fortress was protected by samurai.

To the west of Kobe, Japan, lies the castle Himeji-jo, one of the oldest in the country. Built between the sixteenth and seventeenth centuries, the wooden structure was besieged and even bombed during the Second World War, in 1945. And yet it remains one of the most well-preserved castles in Japan.

The design of Himeji-jo, featuring towers and turrets on every floor linked together with battlements and multiple roofs, gives it an aerial quality. In fact, with its brilliant white walls, it resembles a bird taking flight; hence its nickname, the Castle of the White Heron. The structure encompasses eighty-three buildings.

Himeji-jo's unique architecture hides an ingenious system of defense: two layers of high outer walls, moats filled with water, towers of various sizes, hard-to-reach gates, and a labyrinthine maze of pathways to the main keep. Invaders approaching the castle's donjon could be watched and fired upon with stones and arrows. At the time, political power was held by a shogun ("highest general"), who lived in the castle. This military leader that was backed by samurai, noble warriors charged with defending their country. The samurai were so faithful to their leader that they were prepared to die for him. Himeji-jo is not an isolated castle. It is one of many fortresses forming a solid line of defense throughout the country.

The samurai fought with double-edged swords.

The Potala Palace

Lhasa is the holy capital of Tibetan Buddhism. Built high on a hill, the city's largest monastery seems to touch the sky. The Potala comprises the White Palace, the former living quarters of the Buddhist spiritual leader, and the Red Palace, which houses relics.

Perched on the rooftop of the world, at 11,900 feet, *Lhasa* means "divine city." Since it was founded in the seventh century, the Tibetan capital has always been a major destination for Buddhist pilgrims. Though the holy city boasts a large number of monasteries, the largest and most sacred one is the Potala. A massive structure built high atop a hill, the Potala towers over the rest of the city and is easily recognized from afar by its vivid reds, yellows, and golds.

The Potala is more than just a monastery. Beginning in the seventeenth century, it served as the palace and political center of the government of the Dalai Lama, who was both the spiritual leader of Tibetan Buddhism and the political leader of Tibet. He is believed to be the living incarnation of Buddha, founder of the Buddhist religion. The Dalai Lama hasn't lived in the palace since 1951, the year the Chinese took possession of Tibet.

The Potala is exceedingly large, measuring more than 330 feet in height and comprising eight stories. It served as a residence and place of worship for several thousand monks. Today, however, it is a museum. Visitors come to admire its frescoes depicting the deities and demons of Tibetan Buddism.

Fortunately, there are signs everywhere, because the Potala is quite a maze! The palace is believed to have 999 rooms, in no logical arrangement. A small temple is situated next to a library, for example, and a reception hall takes its place next to an office. This allowed the monks praying in the temple to retreat to the library to study, or those working independently to assemble for a meeting, without having to take the long, dark hallways linking the various parts of the palace together.

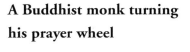

A Buddhist monk turning his prayer wheel

Versailles

The gardens of Versailles were planted with the utmost care, according to the whims of King Louis XIV. Here one finds ponds decorated with sculpted fountains and surrounded by extensive parterres in the warmer seasons. What a change this must have been from the cramped, at times foul-smelling bedrooms inside the palace!

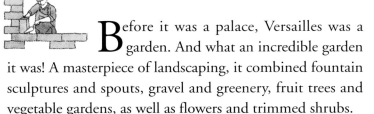

Before it was a palace, Versailles was a garden. And what an incredible garden it was! A masterpiece of landscaping, it combined fountain sculptures and spouts, gravel and greenery, fruit trees and vegetable gardens, as well as flowers and trimmed shrubs.

In the very beginning, however, Versailles was nothing more than a hunting ground composed of marshes and shifting sands. It took the vision of Louis XIV and, after 1662, the talent of André Le Nôtre (gardener, painter, and architect) to transform this inhospitable terrain into a sumptuous park. The garden was constantly changing. Over the course of thirty years, Le Nôtre designed, planted, and replanted the garden parterres, pruned and repruned the trees, changed the layout of the paths, and modified the fountains to the king's liking. Louis XIV was a great nature lover; he liked to stroll through the grounds and keep a close eye on the work being done in the garden. Even the famous Hall of Mirrors inside the palace was conceived in part to reflect the view of the gardens through the windows.

The gardens often served as the backdrop for court festivities, including ballet and theatrical presentations, concerts, and dining by torchlight.

At the time, people came from all over Europe to admire and be inspired by the French gardens, with their symmetrical lines broken only by groves and unique fountains.

King Louis XIV walking with his entourage

The Yukon's Kluane National Park and Reserve

Yukon means "great river" in the language spoken by Eskimos of the Loucheux tribe. Measuring 1,975 miles long, 712 of which are in Canada, the Yukon River crosses the eponymous territory on its way to Alaska. At certain points along the river, huge icebergs appear, formed from glaciers.

Canada's many national parks make up the largest area of protected natural reserves in the world. The Kluane National Park and Reserve, in the Yukon Territory, is gigantic: It covers an area of more than 8,580 square miles and is home to Mount Logan, Canada's highest peak, at an altitude of 19,524 feet. At the foot of the mountains are tremendous ice fields, with spectacularly shaped icebergs. The landscape changes the further one goes into the fertile valleys, which are teeming with trees and plants. Animals are also plentiful in this environment: moose, mouflon, caribou, wolves, lynxes, grizzly and black bears, golden eagles, and salmon, which swim up the river to lay their eggs.

At the end of the nineteenth century, the region's riverbanks were inundated with gold diggers. In 1896, three people discovered gold in one of the area's many streams, spurring a gold rush. Prospectors from all over the continent flocked here to seek their fortune. They sieved alluvial from the bottom of streams to extract small gold nuggets. Around one hundred thousand people dug for gold in the waters of the Yukon, but only a few of them made a fortune.

This prospector is hoping to make his fortune with one big nugget!

Venice

A gondola is indispensable for visiting Venice's Grand Canal, on the Adriatic Sea. This flat-bottomed boat with a high point on each end sails silently over the canals. Although it measures more than thirty feet long and is steered by only one oar, the boat is stable and easy to handle.

Ｉn the fifth century, the inhabitants of the Venetian region, escaping the hordes of barbarians that pervaded the Roman Empire, devastating and looting everything in their path, sought refuge on the islands of a lagoon bordering the coastline. The area wasn't particularly hospitable, with a humid climate, noxious soil, a foul-smelling odor, and an abundance of insects.

Nevertheless, the people managed to make this place livable: They sank thousands of oak tree trunks into the seabed for stability, building a city on stilts above the water and marshes. To channel the rising water, the Venetians built a system of canals linked together by bridges. Today the city's 118 islands are connected by no less than four hundred bridges.

Once their security was ensured, the inhabitants discovered that the lagoon was ideal for fishing and commerce. It was situated in a zone that had a high concentration of fish and was on the maritime route of boats coming from the rich lands of the north toward the Mediterranean. In fact, Venice became such an affluent port city that its power rivaled the maritime might of the Byzantine Empire.

Wealthy merchants built sumptuous palaces on the banks of the Grand Canal, inviting renowned artists to decorate the facades and paint the interiors. Visitors still come from afar to admire these works of art.

The Coral Reef

Belize boasts three atolls and one of the largest coral reefs in the world. The country is also home to the spectacular Blue Hole, a circular abyss measuring 980 feet in diameter and 460 feet in depth, surrounded by coral reef. It's an ideal destination for deep-sea diving!

Coral is a strange, primitive marine animal that scientists have classified among the Anthozoa "animal flowers" because of its roots, shapes, and iridescent colors. There are at least eight hundred species of coral. Some are supple, such as sea anemones, and others are as hard as stone. The latter grow in colonies, slowly forming coral reefs.

These reefs can extend to more than a hundred miles in length. Off the coast of Belize, in the Caribbean Sea, lies the second-largest barrier reef in the world, measuring 185 miles in length. Here, the corals form ring-shaped reefs called atolls, which are spectacular to behold from above, as they look like circles drawn over the sea.

Large numbers of tourists flock to Belize to dive in the reef, home to thousands of fish. In addition, in a multitude of colors and shapes, divers can also admire skate, sea turtles, and even sharks. Another species that calls the reef its home is parrot fish; in fact, the reef protects them from being eaten. Unfortunately, the reverse can't be said for the coral. Parrot fish slowly destroy it with their powerful jaws. But they're not the only menace: Starfish attach themselves to the coral, stifling it; worms, crustaceans, and gastropods (sea snails) pierce the coral in order to take refuge in it; boxfish tear pieces off the reef for food . . . And let's not forget the damage inflicted by humans, who remove whole segments of the coral reef to construct houses, or the pollution that slowly increases the temperature of the water, killing the reef. No doubt about it, coral has a very difficult life!

Sea turtles swim about the coral reef.

The Blue Mosque

The architecture of Istanbul's Blue Mosque is a triumph of space and light: Six tall minarets surround a central dome measuring 141 feet in height and 72 feet in diameter. The interior of the mosque looks like a field of blue flowers.

The so-called Blue Mosque in Istanbul is striking for its large size and its 21,403 handmade tiles from Iznik, a city known for its ceramics. It owes its nickname to the deep blue and turquoise hues of its interior decor.

Floral motifs decorate the mosque's four pillars and walls, from floor to ceiling. Carnations, roses, tulips, hyacinths, and cypresses intertwine, forming a variety of designs seemingly in perpetual motion.

Built between 1609 and 1616, the Blue Mosque is formally named the Mosque of Sultan Ahmet, after the man who commissioned it. Until the end of the nineteenth century, pilgrims leaving for Mecca (the sacred city of Islam in Saudi Arabia) would gather in the courtyard of the mosque on the morning of their departure. From there, a caravan would embark on the pilgrimage—one of the five pillars of Islam defined by the prophet Muhammad. The trip usually took several months. In order to call attention to the sacred role of the mosque as a starting point for pilgrimage, the Sultan Ahmet built it with six minarets instead of the usual four. His decision to build the same number of minarets as on the mosque in Mecca was heavily criticized by religious leaders, who were outraged by the sultan's presumption. The sultan decided to overcome the problem diplomatically, by adding a seventh minaret to the mosque in Mecca, thereby designating its supremacy over all others!

Flowers were the preferred decorative element of ceramic artists during the Ottoman Empire.

The Amazon

The Amazon is home to the largest number of plant species in the world, including a record five thousand species of trees! The gigantic tropical rain forest covers some 2.3 million square miles and receives rain every single day. The Amazon is an ecological site that must be protected for the continued health of our planet.

When the conquistadores arrived in South America in 1500, they were amazed by the rich and refined civilization of the Incas living in the Andes. One legend struck them in particular: the existence of a river so rich in gold that a simple net would suffice to collect it all. The conquistadores flocked to the Marañón River in canoes, searching for the precious metal. When they arrived at the mouth of a yellow-hued river, they thought they had struck gold! Instead, the gold diggers discovered that the river was full of mud and were forced to leave empty-handed.

On their return, they were attacked by long-haired Indian warriors. They named the yellow river the Amazon in reference to the female warriors of Greek mythology. The region through which the river runs, as well as the surrounding forest, was also named the Amazon.

In addition to gold, other rain forest legends involve Indians, plants, and animals. One legend tells the story of a young Indian girl who constantly gazed at the stars and dreamed of becoming one. Thinking that her dream would come true if she could touch the moon—queen of all stars—she climbed a large hill by a lake to get closer to the sky. When night came, the moon's reflection appeared on the lake's surface. While leaning over the side of the lake to touch the moon's reflection, she lost her balance and disappeared in the dark water. The moon, which had affection for the little girl, was so sad to witness her drowning that it transformed her into a beautiful flower floating on the surface of the lake. The flower, a giant, sweet-smelling water lily called Victoria Regia, can be found only in the lakes of the Amazon.

Giant water lilies can be found only in the Amazon rain forest.

133

The Rice Fields of Yunnan

The view from the city of Yuanyang, at an elevation of 5,900 feet, is of terraced rice fields flanking the sides of the mountain. Submerged in water, these rice fields resemble mirrors, reflecting the image of the sky.

Rice is the primary food source for half the world's population, and each society has its own way of growing it. Peasants must often adapt to environments at high altitudes. When necessary, they must cut and level the mountainside to create terraced rice fields. Then they must build low walls to prevent landslides and add soil to level the ground. The skills and know-how of these rice cultivators is extraordinary, especially considering that they often use simple tools and work without the help of animals.

Such is the case for the Hani and Yi people living in the Yunnan province of China. Their rice fields are built tier upon tier up the mountainside, up to 8,200 feet high.

According to legend, the Hani were the first people to create terraces for growing rice. A traditional song recounts how the Mother-Fish created the Hani people at the same time as the earth and the heavens. With fish as their founding fathers, the Hani people have a special connection to water. It is essential in their daily lives, as it allows them to cultivate rice, the food that keeps them alive. Their well-irrigated rice fields bring them three crops a year.

That explains why the Hani pay tribute to water every year during a large ceremony that includes sacrifices, offerings, and processions of people wearing colored costumes through the rice fields.

Rice harvesting is done by hand with help from a sickle.

135

The Galápagos Islands

In 1978, the Galápagos Islands became one of the first natural sites to be inscribed on the World Heritage List. A rapid increase in population jeopardized the islands' ecosystem, threatening the reproduction and sometimes even the existence of species, such as the giant tortoise.

The volcanic islands of the Colón archipelago, in the Pacific Ocean, are called the Galápagos after the giant tortoises that live there. These islands are a true terrestrial paradise, where nature seems to have stood still for four million years.

Only the islands' species have changed, adapting slowly to their environment. The tortoises, for example, differ depending on which island they're from. The Pinta Island tortoises, which have to extend their neck to reach higher shrubs for food, have a long neck and an adapted carapace shape. On the other islands, the tortoises lower their head to feed, which has resulted in a smaller neck. The tortoises all belong to the same family, however, weighing between 440 and 550 pounds, measuring nearly 5 feet long, and living for up to 160 years. Besides varying neck lengths, one tortoise, named Lonesome George, has another major difference: It is the last one on Santa Cruz Island with a saddle-shaped carapace; all the other tortoises have a dome-shaped one.

In 1835, a young English naturalist named Charles Darwin came to the islands to study the local fauna. He was the first to discover that living species adapt to their environment and that species evolve. During his voyage, he discovered that there were fourteen species of tortoises alone!

Birds come by the thousands to nest on the Galápagos Islands.

The Banks of the Danube, Budapest

Budapest became the capital of an independent Hungary in 1867. To mark its newfound political freedom, the Hungarian Parliament (seat of the National Assembly) was built on the bank of the Danube in 1902. Inspired by London's Houses of Parliament, it is an immense structure, built in a neo-Gothic style.

Budapest, the beautiful capital of Hungary, has a large number of monuments and is located on the banks of a long and important waterway, the Danube. The river, which gave Budapest its nickname, Pearl of the Danube, spans 1,771 miles, making it Europe's second largest; it's also the only one to flow from west to east over the uneven terrain. It originates in Germany's Black Forest and snakes through ten countries before emptying into the Black Sea.

Today, 620 miles of the Danube delineate segments of several European countries' borders. During the time of antiquity, it was one of the frontiers between the Roman Empire and the barbarians. Most significantly, it was an extremely navigable waterway, much appreciated by invaders! It was by way of the Danube that the Magyars (nomadic people from Asia) arrived here in the ninth century and founded Hungary. The Mongols, who invaded the young country using the same route, destroyed the city in 1241. Finally, the Ottoman Army conquered Hungary via the Danube in 1526, followed by the Habsburgs—emperors of Austria and kings of Hungary—in 1686!

The Danube has played both a positive and negative role in the history of Budapest. During Roman times, it was a thermal destination, where visitors would come to benefit from the warm waters. In 1838, the banks of the river flooded, devastating the city and causing seventy thousand deaths. In 1867, the Austrian composer Johann Strauss composed a romantic waltz dedicated to the city. Titled "On the Beautiful Blue Danube," the song became known throughout the world.

"On the Beautiful Blue Danube," a waltz, was composed by Johann Strauss.

The Banks of the Seine, Paris

The banks of the Seine have witnessed the entire history of the city of Paris. On the Île de la Cité, the heart of the city, several famous monuments were built, such as Notre-Dame, Sainte-Chapelle, and the Conciergerie, a former palace of the kings of France.

Paris was born on the banks of the Seine, and still today the river serves as the primary reference point in the French capital. The city is divided into two halves: the Right Bank and the Left Bank.

However, the true history of Paris began in between the two banks, when the Gallic Parisii tribe established a settlement on the Île de la Cité to profit from commerce along the river. In 52 BCE, the Romans conquered the Gauls and took over the city, naming it Lutetia Parisiorum. The name was shortened around the year 300 to Paris. The Romans left the Île de la Cité to build their houses and monuments on the Left Bank, on the hills of Sainte-Geneviève, safe from the marshes and the risk of floods. But they continued to profit from the river's prosperous trading route. Later, in the Middle Ages, the "water traders" once again became the reigning masters of Paris. In fact, their coat of arms, represented by a boat with the words "beaten by waves but afloat," was adopted as the symbol of the city.

The Seine has long been known as the economic heart of Paris. Goods and merchandise came and left by way of the river, as did people. Little by little, the city's banks became more populated. Wooden bridges were built to connect the two sides of the river. But an ancient custom required that a toll be paid before passage was allowed. Only monkey trainers could pay "monkey money" to cross the bridge, and only if they could get their monkeys to make funny faces!

Paris took its coat of arms from the one belonging to river merchants during the Middle Ages.

Øresund Bridge

The Øresund Strait separates the Danish city of Copenhagen from the Swedish city of Malmö, to the north. Since July 1, 2000, a bridge and tunnel have connected them. The steel-and-concrete bridge is supported by pillars, and the main section of the bridge is suspended with cables spanning a distance of more than 3,200 feet.

The Øresund Strait is a body of water located between Sweden and Denmark. The Swedes and the Danes decided to link their countries together not just by boat but also by car. The question was, should they build a tunnel or a bridge? Engineers conducted studies, took measurements, and made calculations, before reaching this conclusion: bridge and tunnel! They were preparing to build a true twenty-first-century technological wonder.

Since 2000, travel between Denmark and Sweden via car or train has been possible. Traveling over these 10 miles is quite a unique experience. Starting from Copenhagen, one drives through an underwater tunnel for 2.3 miles, then along a road over an artificial island measuring 2.5 miles in length, and finally, on a bridge spanning 4.9 miles, supported by fifty-two pillars, and held up by four pylons measuring 666 feet high. What's more, the bridge is made up of two levels: The upper level is a highway for cars and trucks, and the lower level is reserved for the railway. What a voyage!

Why are there so many sections? Because on the Danish side, the airport in Copenhagen was built near the water, and it was considered too dangerous to erect a bridge nearby, in the event that an airplane missed a takeoff or landing. The only option was to build an underwater passage. Like the tunnel below the English Channel linking France and Great Britain, the Øresund bridge-tunnel once again underscores humankind's technical triumphs.

A Swedish stamp dating from the bridge's construction

The Ténéré Desert and Aïr Massif

The Ténéré Desert is one of the driest regions in the world, occupying an area 372 miles wide by 930 miles long in Niger. This large plain of sand dunes shaped by the wind stretches out as far as the eye can see. A number of voyagers have lost their lives searching for a way out.

The "desert of deserts": This is the nickname given to the Ténéré, an immense plain of sand in Saharan Africa. The undulating landscape of the area is breathtaking. In some places, the surface is flat, with a sea of sand extending out as far as the horizon; in other places, the dunes are as high as mountain peaks. And in between, there are plateaus and cliffs on which prehistoric people drew images of the animals surrounding them.

Here, the wind is king: It carved the dunes reaching heights of 820 to 985 feet. These are the blue mountains of the Aïr Massif. Caravans of slaves once passed through here on their way to Libya. The blue men of the desert, the Tuareg nomads, still live here. They have long called the Ténéré their home, and they know the dunes and water holes like the back of their hand.

Far from being monotonous, the desert here is actually full of surprises. Nestled at the foot of the cliffs, an oasis appears in the middle of nowhere; farther away, a metal tree emerges from an ocean of sand . . . This strange sculpture was built as a reminder that an actual tree once stood here, not long ago, in the middle of the sand—the only sign of life in this otherwise bleak environment. Besides its symbolic significance, the Ténéré Tree served as a point of reference in the middle of the desert and was even included on maps of the region. Unfortunately, a truck ran over it, which is why it was replaced by a fake one!

Dunes in the blue mountains of the Aïr Massif

The Statue of Liberty

Standing 305 feet high at Liberty Island, the Statue of Liberty looks nothing like a gadget. Yet a certain Mr. Gaget came up with the idea of selling miniature versions of the statue as souvenirs. The miniatures were so popular that they took the name of their inventor, but spelled "gadget"!

Before gracing New York's harbor, the Statue of Liberty dominated the rooftops of the seventeenth arrondissement in Paris, where it was built in a workshop. A French sculptor, Frédéric-Auguste Bartholdi, came up with the idea of creating this 151-foot-tall (from top of base to torch) sculpture in honor of the friendship between France and the United States and in commemoration of the centennial of the United States' July 4, 1776, independence. The statue, formally titled *Liberty Enlightening the World*, celebrates the values of knowledge, liberty, and democracy. The broken chains at the foot of the statue symbolize the crushing of slavery.

Getting this project off the ground took plenty of energy and dedication! First, money had to be raised. Bartholdi came up with the idea of exhibiting various parts of the statue to attract generous donations. He brought one of the statue's arms with him on a trip to Philadelphia in 1876. But given that the index finger alone measured eight feet, he traveled with more than just a suitcase! Luckily, the statue was made up of hundreds of individual copper pieces that could be transported fairly easily. The exhibited arm piqued the curiosity of a large number of Americans, who were anxious to see more of this statue that was already being heavily touted by the press.

In 1878, Bartholdi used the occasion of the World's Fair, which attracted a large number of countries, to display the statue's completed head, measuring seventeen feet. He even organized a fund-raising dinner in one of the statue's sandals. And it worked! Money poured in. Once completed, the statue was reduced to individually numbered pieces, packed in 214 crates, and shipped to New York, where it was welcomed by an enthusiastic crowd and became a symbol of liberty for people everywhere.

The Statue of Liberty's face was modeled on Bartholdi's mother!

Brasília

Brasília, the very young and modern capital of Brazil, was inaugurated in 1960. Its cathedral was built in the purest of styles: The interior is flooded with light, thanks to a magnificent stained-glass window. On the ceiling, statues of angels seem to have descended directly from heaven.

In 1956, the president of Brazil founded a new capital to replace Rio de Janeiro. By situating the new capital in the semiarid central part of the country, the government hoped to promote the development of the region, which at that time was very poor. Until then, a vast majority of the population lived in cities along the coast.

The new capital, Brasília, became a masterpiece of modernist design. The architect of the city's modern projects was named Lucio Costa. Along with Oscar Niemeyer, who built the city's many landmarks, he created a capital of 600,000 inhabitants in a record four years! Costa imagined Brasília as a gigantic bird with open wings, flying toward the southeast. The body of the bird contains administrative buildings, while residential areas extend out along the wings.

Distances within the city are considerable. Brasília is home to the longest avenue in the world, which forms the body of the bird. This six-lane avenue is more than 820 feet wide, with a park area in the middle. Government buildings can be seen on either side of the avenue, culminating in a square with more political buildings in the head of the bird. The Chamber of Deputies looks like a dome, and the Federal Senate looks like an inverted dome. Between the two, the Palace of the Congress is a skyscraper made up of two twin towers. Geometric concrete structures dominate the landscape: The Boa Vontade church resembles a pyramid, whereas the cathedral is more symbolic, shaped like a crown of thorns.

The project for a new capital dates back to the independence of Brazil, in the 1820s. The bird is a symbol of this independence, acquired after centuries of Portuguese control.

The cathedral is shaped like a crown of thorns.

The Northern Lights

The aurora borealis, or northern lights, is only visible on Earth from Scandinavia, Greenland, Iceland, Canada, Alaska, and Siberia. It is composed of streams of colorful bright lights, mostly green or red, that dance across the night sky.

A polar aurora is called "borealis" in the northern hemisphere and "australis" in the southern hemisphere. It is a natural phenomenon that occurs in the sky only in regions close to the poles and only at night. Auroras are the results of explosions in the center of the sun. Highly charged solar particles from space rain down over the atmosphere, forming dense clouds of light that strengthen in the wind. The array of colors emitted depends on the altitude at which they occur, which can be anywhere from 50 to 250 miles above the earth's surface.

Common in Greenland and all the Nordic countries, an aurora borealis can sometimes last several hours. A person seeing this celestial vision for the first time will be spellbound by the dazzling display of colors across the sky.

The ancient Greeks understood the aurora borealis as an atmospheric occurence, whereas the Romans, three hundred years later, attributed it to angry gods and viewed the streams of light as omens. Similarly, in the Middle Ages, the aurora borealis struck fear in people's minds, as they believed the lights were a warning of a forthcoming catastrophe. Fear was the result of the population's ignorance. It wasn't until the seventeenth century that scholars started to observe the strange phenomenon and discovered its solar origin.

For the Inuit and Indian populations living in the polar regions, the aurora borealis is viewed as either dead spirits playing in the sky; the dancing spirits of animals such as salmon, seals, or reindeer; or reflections of light from torch-carrying giants!

Some view the lights as torches carried by giants.

PHOTOGRAPHY CREDITS